Work Remotely

Martin Worner is a co-founder and Head of Product at Confio, building trade, a blockchain aimed at regulated financial institutions. He has worked in various product and technology roles in blockchain since 2017, mostly in remote teams. He has a capital markets and technology background, initially working at UBS, Morgan Stanley, and then starting and growing a company with technology expertise, serving investment banks, funds and hedge funds. He has worked with teams around the world, and was an early adopter of remote working. He lives in the UK and works with a fully remote team.

Anastasia Tohmé is a global talent acquisition and HR expert. She has been recruiting for numerous companies expanding their businesses, and has been setting up HR departments and growing teams in fields such as technology, blockchain, real estate and financial services across six continents. She currently runs the international talent acquisition team at Global Upside Corporation, a leading global services company, and lectures 'HR Management' and 'Managing Remote Teams' at Geneva Business School. She holds an MBA from IE Business School and a dual degree in HRM from McGill University and Université de Montréal. She lives in Spain and has been fully remote since 2018.

Anastasia Tohmé
and Martin Worner

Work Remotely

BUSINESS

PENGUIN BUSINESS EXPERTS

UK | USA | Canada | Ireland | Australia
India | New Zealand | South Africa

Penguin Business Experts is part of the Penguin Random
House group of companies whose addresses can
be found at global.penguinrandomhouse.com.

 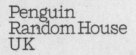

Penguin
Random House
UK

First published 2021
001

Copyright © Anastasia Tohmé and Martin Worner, 2021

The moral right of the copyright holders has been asserted

Text design by Richard Marston
Set in 11.75/14.75 pt Minion Pro
Typeset by Jouve (UK), Milton Keynes
Printed and bound in Great Britain by Clays Ltd,
Elcograf S.p.A.

The authorized representative in the EEA is
Penguin Random House Ireland, Morrison
Chambers, 32 Nassau Street, Dublin D02 YH68

A CIP catalogue record for this book is available
from the British Library

ISBN: 978–0–241–48211–7

Follow us on LinkedIn: https://www.linkedin.
com/company/penguin-connect/

Contents

Part 3: Self-care and Self-organization

Introduction

Since the modern office emerged, remote working has been the exception rather than the norm. A 2018 survey found that only 3 per cent of employees in America worked from home more than half of the time. But in just over a year, with the arrival of the global coronavirus pandemic in 2020, thousands of companies were forced to close offices and many millions of people had to work from home. In the first wave of the virus in the UK in April 2020, nearly 50 per cent of those in employment began to work away from the office. Companies all over the world are embracing remote working. Jack Dorsey, the CEO of Twitter, has moved all jobs that don't require a physical presence in the office to remote positions. And many more have followed suit. Traditional offices are now a thing of the past. To reap the benefits of remote work, we need to examine what the workplace means and recognize the opportunities that flexible work offers. We must become more innovative and proactive in our approach and bring about greater conscious and rigorous experimentation with our ways of working. Remote has become the new normal. And it's here to stay.

It's time to rethink how, where and why we work. It's time to join the work remotely revolution.

The case for remote working

Widen your work horizons

Without the geographical constraints of a central office, many employers are able to tap into a larger talent pool beyond the local labour market. In a survey of hiring managers, 64 per cent said they were now more likely to consider remote candidates for a position, while the majority found the virtual hiring process a cost-effective form of talent acquisition. Companies can channel the money no longer needed for rent into offering higher wages and attracting more talented staff. No longer being tied down to a particular city or location means employees can pursue their careers while still remaining close to their family and social networks. A highly attractive concept according to one study which found that respondents would require to be paid $24,000 more to no longer be near family.

Remote working offers a more level playing field for those hampered by invisible barriers, as traditional discriminatory factors such as race, age, gender, class and disability are reduced in the hiring process. Simply taking away the physical and financial barriers involved in commuting can have a huge impact on those without easy access to an office, or who cannot afford or may not be able to do so. Once in the virtual workspace, employees from minorities experience less prejudice, one study found, due to a focus on results rather than traditional hierarchical and political factors.

Increase your productivity

Several recent studies have confirmed what most of us already knew: working at home boosts productivity among workers. One investigation of over 13,000 global businesses revealed that

85 per cent found that their teams were more productive when working remotely.[1] In 2015, American Express launched a global telecoms network to deliver their customer care. They wanted to attract the best talent in the sector while still managing a high volume of requests across their network. When the company carried out research on their employees' productivity, they found that the remote teleworkers took 26 per cent more calls than their colleagues working in Amex's central office, which resulted in an output increase of 43 per cent.[2] Each remote worker was worth almost 50 per cent more than their office-based counterpart.

Benefit from a happy and healthy workforce

For many employees, working from home means they have greater flexibility and autonomy to plan their day, more time for hobbies and interests, for socializing with family and friends and looking after pets. With hours saved by not commuting, workers can dedicate more time to exercise and to preparing healthier meals. One study found 77 per cent of employees claimed that working from home had improved their overall health and wellbeing. A survey by KBC Bank showed that work–life balance has increased by 87 per cent; 83 per cent of those interviewed said that they can work with greater concentration; 72 per cent feel less stressed at work; 68 per cent are more motivated; and 62 per cent can organize their work better.[3] The study also stated that there are benefits for employers too, with employee retention up 76 per cent for workers with flexible work options.

Embrace new leadership techniques

Switching to a virtual system of communication has eroded workplace hierarchical structures and traditional political systems within companies. The ability to Zoom call into our colleagues' living rooms has broken down social barriers; it can be positive to realize that our managing directors have families, homes to run and personal struggles too. Many organizations are embracing a shift towards a more humane, relatable form of leadership.

Live rent free

Grand offices in glass skyscrapers on premium central city plots cost companies millions every year. In New York, office space costs, on average, $14,800 per employee annually, including cleaning services, food and catering fees and taxes.[4] Skift Inc., a media company, has saved $600,000 annually by giving up its midtown Manhattan offices and co-working spaces for the London-based employees, including the expensive utilities.[5] Saving on significant outgoing costs like this frees up money that can be spent on attracting talent or upgrading technology.

Lower your carbon footprint

If those who have a work-from-home compatible job and a desire to work remotely did so just half the time, greenhouse gas reduction would be the equivalent to taking the entire New York state workforce off the road.[6] In 2015, Xerox reported its teleworkers drove 92 million fewer miles, saving 4.6 million gallons of petrol, reducing carbon dioxide emissions by nearly 41,000 metric tons.[7]

These are just some of the many benefits that can be harnessed from the remote work revolution. This book will show how both individuals and organizations can maximize the benefits and get the best results from working flexibly.

Of course, there are still those sceptical of the move to remote working. Some employees thrive on the opportunity to connect with colleagues face-to-face and network within the office environment. Others like the structure and routine that the working day offers. Many don't have a home environment conducive to work and some worry that colleagues being able to see their living spaces may lead to social comparisons which can favour those in a more privileged situation. This book will guide you through the challenges of remote working, show you how to recognize the opportunities and pitfalls that it has brought about and enable you to become more innovative and productive in your approach to collaboration, performance evaluation, rewards, hiring, training and culture.

Work Remotely came about from our first-hand experience of working together in a remote-first company at a time when remote work was still the exception: Anastasia led HR and Martin led Product. We combined our knowledge with extensive research to produce the most complete guide for anyone aiming to progress in their career working remotely. Our goal was to set out the best practices of remote work and equip every reader with the skills they need to succeed as they work remotely.

The book is divided into three parts: Working in a Remote Team, Managing a Remote Team and Self-care and Self-organization. Part One, Working in a Remote Team, examines the ways we can benefit from remote working; how we can communicate, collaborate and create remotely and use technology as our toolkit. It reveals how to mitigate the downsides of remote working, nurture a culture of diversity and inclusion, and the importance of open discussion and conflict resolution in a remote setting. Part Two, Managing a Remote Team, explores how to bring together your team virtually, the ways in which managing remotely differs from managing in the office, how to set up and manage processes effectively in your team, and the methods to measure success by setting goals and gathering data on progress. There are also useful guidelines on hiring, onboarding and offering promotions. Part Three, Self-care and Self-organization, details practical advice on how to take care of yourself as you work remotely. *Work Remotely* is a handbook; you can choose to read it from start to finish or jump to a specific section you need help with straightaway.

History of the office as a central place of work

The office has been in existence for a long time, serving as an administrative place for the centralized power of the state, a central function where employees processed necessary paperwork. Notable examples would be the Medici's Palazzo Uffizi in Florence or the Bank of England. The roots of collective work in a central workspace stem from the evolution of the factory in eighteenth-century Europe. Prior to this, city people worked in the city, rural people worked in their homes or workshops attached to their homes. The advent of factories led to mass migration to towns as work needed to be centralized. Mass migration to cities continues to this day throughout the world. In 2018, according to the United Nations Economic and Social Council, thirty-three megacities hosted 13 per cent of the global urban population and, by 2030, the number of megacities is projected to increase to forty-one with 14 per cent of urban dwellers worldwide residing in megacities.

With the invention of the telegraph and the telephone, offices could be situated away from the home or factory while control over production and distribution to other markets could still be retained. Other new technologies such as the light bulb, the typewriter and the use of calculating machines allowed large amounts of information to be accumulated and processed faster and more efficiently than before. The concentration of wealth required an ever greater proportion of an increasingly literate population to work in the new 'white collar factories'. In Chicago, technologies such as the steel frame and the lift enabled the construction of office buildings higher than previously possible to generate maximum income from the site. This profit-driven logic came to define the skyscrapers of Chicago and New York by the early twentieth century, and later Dubai and Hong Kong, to name just a few. Eventually, entire cities and urbanizations, from suburbs and residential neighbourhoods to highways and complex transportation systems, were built around commercial and financial districts, which contributed to a great extent to real estate booms around the world.

As the surge of the industrial era led to mass migration to cities, new problems started to surface, primarily congestion in urban centres across the globe. According to the RingCentral blog, on average, any worker around the world loses about a month of each year commuting back and forth to work. Quite apart from the stress endured in traffic and the costs of owning and running a vehicle, the daily carbon emissions adversely affect the environment. It didn't take long before scholars started questioning the way we work and considering other more efficient systems. The terms 'telework' and 'tele-commuting', both frequently used today, were coined by the author Jack Nilles back in the early 1970s. Along with his co-authors F. Roy Carlson Jr, Paul Gray and Gerhard J. Hanneman, Nilles examined the idea of moving the work to the workers instead of moving the workers to work. They argued that congested cities lead to communication inefficiencies in the workplace. At that time, the personal computer had not yet been invented, so there was no way to relocate work to homes.

In the last three decades, offices have moved to open-plan layouts and with that came a drop in productivity[8] chiefly due to rising noise levels and distractions from passers-by. Over time, conversations have been replaced by internal instant messaging communication tools such as Slack, Teams or Skype, resulting in a constant messaging culture, so that we are now as likely to use our laptops to send a message as we are to walk over to a colleague's desk.

The office still functions as a place where we can meet, discuss projects and share a common culture. But the reality is that we are all so busy with our separate tasks that finding time and a place to meet is a challenge. We are often spread out over multiple floors, buildings and even countries. Proximity does not necessarily equate to a meshed team, working together at all times.

Looking at the modern office-based organization today, with people working in silos, headphones on, you must ask yourself: do we really need to be in an office? If the way we are working isn't working, does this present an opportunity to rethink how we operate? What are the arguments for remote working, either fully remote or a blend of remote and onsite? The compelling argument for remote working has become possible through a combination of the available technology, such as reliable desktop video calling, cloud applications and high-speed connectivity, with the realization that there is a global talent pool which can be drawn on, and a cultural move to demand more control of where and how people want to work. There are challenges with remote working as it is different from office-based work; however, once you know where to focus and what needs to be put in place, there is a great foundation to build on.

Part 1   Working in a Remote Team

1 How We Work

Getting to know your team

Whether you're part of a team in a big company or a freelancer brought on to a short-term project, getting to know your team is vital to your success. In the next section we will look at some of the various tribes, how they work, what motivates them and how you can adapt to get the best results while working with them remotely.

The remote tribes

If you try to imagine a remote worker, it will probably be a picture of a young Macbook-toting software programmer that will pop into your head. But the reality is that remote workers are not a homogeneous group and can be any age and from a broad range of industries. Let's look at some of the different remote tribes.

The corporate escapee

Working From Home, abbreviated to WFH, and otherwise known as 'Home Office', 'Teleworking' or 'Flexi-working', is now widely used in the corporate world. Companies typically offer one day per week when employees can work from their home or a location of their choice, saving commuting time or offering workers the chance to get away for the weekend. Many businesses use this as an opportunity to save on desk space and keep staff rotating on a one-day WFH schedule. People have started to build the WFH arrangements into their lives, such as WFH on Tuesdays to pick up children from school, or to fit in a dentist's appointment. In a survey from 2019 by Regus, 62 per cent of firms globally reported that they had a flexible working policy in place.[1]

An element of WFH is now part of normal corporate life; what will vary is the ratio of days in the office.

Working à la carte

This tribe is a subset of the WFH-ers. It is a result of the high cost of cities that people are prepared to commute further distances in the search for space and an affordable place to live. The *Guardian* newspaper published a heatmap in 2016 illustrating the percentage of people by region commuting to London. It showed pockets across England and Wales from where people officially commute to London.[2] These are the people you see on the early trains on a Monday morning with their laptops and a slightly larger weekend bag. They get to work later than everyone else but will work longer in the evening to make up for it. They either have a small apartment near work, or share a house with others; in some cases, they have made an arrangement through one of the many online marketplaces to stay at someone's house while they are away for the week. They stay until either Wednesday or Thursday night and then catch the train back to where they live and work from home for the remainder of the week. In extreme cases, the train is swapped for a flight, if the person works in another country for the three or four days required.

John, a management consultant based in Cornwall, UK

John is a keen surfer. As a student in Cornwall, he had spent his summers working in bars to fund his passion, and once he started working he spent as many weekends as he could visiting the surfing beaches. Eventually he and his partner (also an avid surfer) decided they would move to a village near Newquay, while he continued to work in London three days a week and worked at home for the remaining two. His partner was luckier, having found a fully remote job.

John's week begins on Monday at 05.00 when he drives to London, getting in around 10.30. He rents a room from a friend who lives near his office, which means he can get to work early on Tuesday and stay later to maximize his time at work.

After his day in the office on Wednesday, he sets off towards the end of the evening rush hour and gets home some time after midnight.

Thursday and Friday are spent working from home, and in the lighter evenings he is able to catch some waves after work.

Digital nomads

Digital nomads are knowledge- or information-based workers who are employed by organizations but choose to live in, and work from, a variety of places. For example, Kate is employed by a London-based design studio but lives in a house in southern Spain in summer and in the Alps during winter. The appeal of being a digital nomad is the chance to travel the world and live in beautiful, affordable places while doing a job you enjoy. There are websites, such as Nomad List or Nomadific, along with dozens of Facebook pages, which guide the nomads to the best co-working places to live and the cultural events available. It does raise many questions, such as the work rights in different countries, where you pay your taxes and what visas you might need. Is it really possible to chill out in Goa in winter and work for a business based in Amsterdam through an Estonian service company without needing an Indian work permit or paying any local tax? This is still a relatively new phenomenon, so the obligations and rights of digital nomads, as well as the companies employing them, are still not clear. For example, in 2021, Mark Zuckerberg, CEO of Facebook, asked all staff working abroad to notify the company of their location and adjusted their salary accordingly depending on the local economy and currency.

Hommies

This category of remote worker, in contrast to the nomad, is someone who has a strong tie to a location. While the hommie could relocate to a big city or to a region where businesses cluster, the connection to a certain location, such as having extended family close by or simply wanting to live in a particular place, keeps them there.

There are factors in city living, such as high rents, which make people reconsider their plans, and there are tempting places such as the beaches of Bali, or attractive schemes such as the recent one to repopulate towns in Sicily, with houses being sold for €1.[3]

Hommies can be seen as a positive trend for rural communities and smaller towns which have suffered decades of depopulation with the young migrating to the cities, and they can help to maintain diverse communities.

Hommies are less keen to travel for meetings, retreats or company events as their attachment to where they live is strong. The hommie tribe is thus a natural remote worker, through choice.

CASE STUDY

José, a software engineer based in Ponferrada, Spain

After finishing university, José went to London to find a job in software engineering, leaving behind his home town, Ponferrada in Spain, where there were few opportunities in his field. But, after building a career and working remotely in the USA, Berlin and Paris, José came back to his home town to be near his family and bring up his children. Completely comfortable with remote working, he has an office set up at home and he can join his family for lunch and take his children to their football matches. He is accustomed to using technology to communicate with his team and is able to take advantage of his flexible arrangement to balance work with his home life.

Gig workers

The term 'gig worker'[4] includes independent contractors, online platform workers, on-call workers or temporary workers. In short, the term is a catch-all for non-traditional workers. Gig workers are specialists who find work on websites which match companies or individuals looking for people to do a job with those qualified to do it. The work can be done 'by the hour' or on a project basis. We will not be covering gig workers such as car drivers or bicycle couriers as these jobs are not comparable to the remote work being discussed.

The gap between the gig knowledge workers and a remote

team is narrow: both work remotely by choice and, similar to outsourcing, the gig workers can be brought in according to the business needs and scaled back when no longer required. Gig workers establish their reputation and ranking on the websites and will typically build a portfolio of companies they work with. For a company there are advantages in having a pool of people they trust to do a good job, the downside being that gig workers are not always available as they have multiple clients. There is a role for gig workers in occasional project work, such as asking a graphic designer to create a logo or define company branding which may change infrequently. In such a scenario gig workers may offer the best solution.

Shared values and objectives

Once you've identified how each member of your team likes to work, it's crucial to ensure everyone is working together towards a unified goal and to make sure the objectives and priorities of the company and team are clear and easily accessible for all members. Everyone should be aware of both the company's vision and its mission statement.

The company vision

The company vision is a statement defining the company and where it aims to develop. This can be ambitious but must be crystal clear. For example, LinkedIn states: 'Create economic opportunity for every member of the global workforce', and Facebook urges: 'Connect with friends and the world around you on Facebook.'[5]

The mission statement

The mission statement is more about what the organization does and can be thought of dealing with today. An example of a mission statement, from Sony, the electronics company, defines its purpose as: 'Fill the world with emotion, through the power of creativity and technology.'[6] Not every company's mission needs to be as vague or corporate, or as flippant as Google's famous 'Do no evil', but there is a serious point, that it is particularly important for remote workers to unite around a common mission. A more grounded mission statement comes from Clif Bar[7]: 'We're working to run a different kind of company: The kind of place we'd want to work, that makes the kind of food we'd like to eat, and that strives for a healthier, more sustainable world – the kind of world we'd like to pass on to our children. And those aren't just words. They're our mission statement.' The day-to-day mission of the company is unambiguous and easy for the staff to understand and embrace.

Once the vision and mission are clearly articulated, it is handy to have them documented in a place where people can find them. It would be highly advisable to create a company handbook that contains a company's goals, values, policies and procedures and is accessible to all employees and shared with new hires on their starting date. The next step is translating this into the more practical perspective of shared values and objectives. A great way for the company objectives to be reinforced and refreshed on a quarterly basis is for the CEO to do a presentation to the employees on what has been achieved – aligned to the mission – and where the company is heading – the vision. Nick Francis, CEO of Help Scout,[8] a remote customer care company, delivers an all-hands-on meeting with his team leads, preparing slides which he collates and uses to update all staff.

The shared values and objectives reflect the company's vision and mission and focus on how we work with each other, our customers and suppliers.

- The tone is set by the leadership team and explicitly shared by the managers. Practically, this means having clear policies around expected behaviour, and managers need to remind staff of what their policies are and where to find them. An example would be clear guidelines around harassment and bullying, including how these are defined, the reporting procedures and the consequences.

- Cultivate an open and transparent way of working by including all employees and sharing information. Regular all-hands-on meetings are a great way to share the highlights of what is going on in the company and to encourage questions and provide answers.

- Set the company values on the environment with an objective to minimize the carbon footprint and detail the practical steps to implement this, such as green travel policies, offsetting CO_2 impact and a purchasing policy around recycled materials.

Creating and celebrating a culture of diversity

Remote teams are often in different countries and will need to navigate cultural differences and diversity.

When considering cultural issues, we see, for example in patriarchal societies, that there is a tendency not to challenge a manager, whereas in other cultures where more direct communication is the norm the way a person challenges a manager may seem rude. If you ask one of your team members in India to do something, even if there is a better way to do it, you will not be challenged because the 'boss is always right'. By contrast, if you ask one of your team members in Ukraine, the challenge could be more direct than you expect. Both attitudes can be changed, but it has to be done incrementally by constructive feedback.

Cultural diversity involves being aware of and celebrating differences. For example, a German view on punctuality may vary from a Southern European one. Similarly, if a team settles on English as a common language, there may be miscommunications and nuances lost in translation. The worst offenders in a multinational team are usually native English speakers who confuse non-native English speakers with obscure idioms or use cultural references that have no meaning outside their own country.[9] For example: 'Our new web application was launched with a Marmite home page' is a cultural reference to an advertisement with the slogan 'Love it or hate it.' Not being direct, for instance saying 'We were fairly disappointed, in this quarter's sales' when you mean you were very disappointed, is confusing. A clearer 'We are disappointed in this quarter's sales figures' would be more valuable to non-native speakers.

Creating a monoculture or 'global model' is not the answer. Increasingly, people are demanding to work in culturally diverse organizations, as cultural diversity is something to be celebrated and brings valuable perspective to projects. In a Glassdoor article, 'What Job Seekers Really Think About Your Diversity and

Inclusion Stats', 67 per cent of those surveyed said that a diverse workforce is an important factor when they are considering a job.[10] There should, however, be some ground rules to ensure everyone is treated with respect.

- Make a clear statement that discrimination based on gender, age, race, religion or sexual orientation is not acceptable

- Establish a definition of what is meant by bullying or harassment, namely behaviour that makes someone feel intimidated or offended. Examples include spreading malicious rumours, unfair treatment, picking on or regularly undermining someone and denying someone training or promotion opportunities[11]

- Encourage those running meetings to ensure that everyone has the right to express their views (within the boundaries of discrimination) and the opportunity to speak without interruption

- Agree on a common language to be used in spoken and written form

Drawing up the rules should be a team effort and should start with each member of the team writing down what is important to them. The lists should then be merged and prioritized, ensuring inclusivity. Running a series of short 'getting to know each other' presentations by each person, saying what is special about the place they live in and how they work, would enable the whole team to learn and acquire a better understanding about other countries, their customs and culture.

Who is who?

We have set the cultural rules, the shared values and objectives of the company; the next step is to define the 'who does what' and bring clarity around roles and responsibilities.

The most effective companies have strong communication between the leadership and the workforce and this stems from having a clear organizational structure. Granularity in the structure means that there is clarity in the roles, and specifically in what a team member is expected to do and where their responsibilities lie.

To maintain a strong organizational structure, when a role is created and filled, you must ensure the expectations of the role are well defined, and it must be reviewed from time to time as almost all roles evolve as the company grows. When defining roles, it should be clear who the person reports to and what the person's responsibility is, thus ensuring they fit in with the rest of the organization.

While traditional companies may have a rigid hierarchy, there is room for a more dynamic definition of responsibilities in remote teams. For example, one person may be identified to take responsibility for the duration of a project and this could switch. If you are looking to have a more vibrant team, then the organization must set up rotation programmes where team members can enjoy different responsibilities, but this requires some preparation and clear communication.

Now that you know why it is important for everyone in the remote team to be clear about who does what, the next challenge is to establish who reports to whom. The easiest way to do this is to create a live or online repository of short biographies of all team members with a description of what they do, their areas of expertise and even a small wall of fame outlining their successes. It should be recognized that not everybody is comfortable writing their biography or detailing their recent achievements, so it is better to choose one team member as an 'internal journalist' or bring in a specialist who can set up the templates and document the initial interviews.

GitLab[12] publish their whole organization chart online. It's interactive, and each person has a photo and a short description of what they do. MailerLite[13] have a simplified version, with name, photo and which department each person works in. Both GitLab and MailerLite go beyond what is needed by making this public, but it fits with their ethos of transparency.

Why six is a magic number

Katherine Klein[14] at the Wharton School, University of Pennsylvania, came up with the idea that six is the magic number for the size of a team, but, while it is nice to have a simple answer, the truth is that somewhere between four and nine is best, with six being the average. The magic number of six is very relevant to remote teams who meet on video calls, because more than that may risk communication being dominated by one or two while the others idly surf the net and stop contributing. The decrease in productivity proportional to team size is known as the 'Ringelmann effect'.[15] Ringelmann's study, where he coined the term 'social loafing',[16] involved an experiment with teams pulling on a rope, during which he discovered that adding more people to the team did not increase the efficacy of the team pulling. Jeff Bezos, of Amazon, came up with the theory that the best team size is the one that can be fed by two pizzas,[17] and believes larger teams are less efficient as they require more administration.

The team size of six remote workers can work well without one being a dedicated lead, as long as the structure of communication and meetings is well established. A criticism of smaller team sizes is that it imposes a cost on the business by having to employ more staff in managerial or team leader positions and the cost of these people is higher. The reality is that there is a mix of people in the team, with some juniors, some mid-level members and some senior in terms of experience. This is healthy, as the juniors learn from the more experienced, and senior people benefit also because having to explain things to juniors helps them clarify and organize their own thoughts.

The number six does not stop with the productive team turning out code, documents or designs; six of these teams can be managed by one person, and six of these managers of teams of six can be managed by one person (who could also manage an additional five people). You get the picture! It scales well and keeps the teams effective. From a remote working aspect, this level of management and grouping helps keep things together and ensures communication flows.

Collective knowledge

Collective knowledge is the information about an organization held within that organization, and this covers not only how things work but how processes are carried out, the shortcuts used and a map detailing where the expertise lies.

Building the collective knowledge in a remote team means making sure the knowledge, know-how and processes are documented, stored and shared seamlessly. Each team member must be able to retrieve the material they need in a way that is intuitive.

How do we go about building the collective knowledge so everyone can find it? The example below illustrates how a remote web agency does it.

- The shared drive has all the recordings of meetings, stored in clearly labelled sub-folders.

- A collection of videos from the web developers is held in the web-knowledge folder, recording the talks or presentations by the developers with screen-shares to walk people through a topic relevant to the languages in use.

- The team folders are for research papers, meeting notes and archives where old files are kept for context.

- The online or cloud whiteboards are used for collaboration and collecting ideas or getting creative. The outputs of the virtual whiteboards with annotations are filed in the ideas folders.

- Finally, the marketing drives have the company branding resources (colour palettes, font guides and logos in all shapes and sizes). In addition, there are all the latest customer-facing materials, from simple introduction to more detailed papers, and a public drive with some video explainers which can be shared with prospective customers.

What is the perfect collective knowledge base?

In the early 2000s there was a buzz about the new role of Chief Knowledge Officer.[18] The idea was to have a person in the leadership teams of corporates responsible for the gathering and developing of the key asset of the company, namely knowledge. While this role is less fashionable now, it did raise a valuable point about collecting and making the knowledge within a company easily accessible to all.

TOP TIP

Appoint a person on your team to be responsible for designing your documentation systems and communicating them to the rest of the team.

2 How We Communicate

The rules of engagement

Communication is the most important element in creating a successful remote team. Without the intonations and gestures that you get from face-to-face communication, remote workers have to develop heightened virtual communication skills, which can be learned and improved through practice. In this section we will look at some of the ways you can do this.

First, the team should work together to define some communication conventions. Examples of these are:

- All internal communication should be through a messaging application, such as Teams or Slack.

- Email should be used only for external communications.

- WhatsApp or equivalent should be used for emergencies only.

- Pick up the phone or click the video link when possible.

These communication conventions should be clearly defined and accessible to all, especially new members of staff. It goes without saying that the right tools to communicate effectively must be in place. Team members must know how to articulate their messages clearly using the appropriate technology. There is a place for email, instant messaging, video calls and other forms of communication, but each team will have their own way of working that suits their needs, so finding the best way to work together is the first step towards effective communication.

Thiago Duarte, a lead developer at Toggl, a remote first company, explains in an interview with Twist that they use Slack and Zoom as their prime tools to improve communication in the remote setting.[1] Making clear which tools are being used is a good first step, but you also need to publish a guide on which one to use in which circumstances.

Basecamp, a successful remote software company, have developed a complete guide to internal communication describing the how, where, why and when to communicate. This guide acts as a rule of thumb and comprises a collection of general principles they apply when communicating across the company, whether it be between teammates or within departments. The guide's thirty principles create boundaries and place the communication culture prioritizing asynchronous communication over real-time.

Examples of these principles are:

- 'Speaking only helps who is in the room, writing helps everyone'

- 'Meetings are the last resort, not the first option'

- 'Five people in a room for an hour isn't a one-hour meeting, it's a five-hour meeting. Be mindful of the tradeoffs'

- 'The expectation of immediate response is toxic'

- 'Poor communication creates more work'

The quickest route to action

Finding the shortest path between the decision-maker and the person carrying out the task or activity is especially important in a remote setting and is a key to effective communication. In a remote setting, if there are many people involved, this can be complicated by time zone differences, or because people may simply be unaware of the importance of a decision that needs to be taken.

In the workplace setting, it is much easier to get quick answers as you can see if someone is free or busy. In a remote setting, where the team is not visible, it becomes more of a challenge. When relying on chat applications, it is tempting to send messages to lots of people to get a quick answer on the premise that 'someone will answer'. However, this slows everything down as it distracts people.

Some strategies can help you become efficient at getting answers:

- Send a quick reply to acknowledge that a message has been seen. For example, replying 'Hi, seen this, got a deadline for finance, I will get back to you in thirty mins', reassures the sender that their message has been seen.

- Be disciplined with your calendar and keep it up to date so that people know when you are free.

- Set a virtual 'office hour' in your calendar every week so employees can drop in and ask questions.

Effective video calls

In the post-coronavirus world, the video call is king. The bad call is very easy to recognize: the two-hour slot in the calendar, twenty attendees and a poor internet connection. But what makes a great video call? Here are some ideas:

- The kit: a good camera and microphone are a must. There are two types of microphone: the omni-directional and the cardioid. The omni-directional will pick up everything around it including all the background noise generated if you are in a room with other people. A cardioid microphone will pick up the speaker and not the background.

- The guest list: who is invited is important. Only invite the people who need to be there to make decisions or those who are required for a Q&A session. If anyone is being included for 'information', they do not need to be present provided you make sure the documentation is promptly produced and you invite them for a follow-up call if there are items that need further clarification. We still have the habit of setting up calls for an hour because that was how long physical meetings used to last, as people had to go from one place to another to attend. Today, there is no reason why a video call can't be fifteen minutes long.

- Follow the agenda: this may seem obvious, but you should provide an agenda and any relevant documents, videos or images beforehand so people know exactly what the call is about and how long each point will take.

- Who's in charge? A video call needs a good chairperson or mediator to ensure that it follows the agenda and that diversions are prevented and follow-up sessions are scheduled where appropriate.

- Who's watching the clock? It often helps to have a separate attendee ensuring that the allotted time for each agenda point is observed. If the meeting overruns, then outstanding points can be rearranged.

- Who's taking minutes? Any action points have to be followed up, so a good record of these is a must.

QUICK TIPS

▶ A quality internet connection is very important for communication. There is nothing worse in a video call than a participant's screen freezing or their voice breaking up. Plan ahead if you are expecting a call, and make sure you are in a place with a good mobile or WiFi signal.

▶ If you have a messy room or an untidy book collection, there are tools in video-calling applications that can blur or add a background to make you look more professional.

▶ If you are using slides, then it is better to share in presentation mode so people can see them in full screen. Allow time for a run through to avoid any technical problems on the day.

▶ When you are in screen-sharing mode, don't forget to stop sharing when you stop presenting. It would be very embarrassing if someone switched to the messaging app, forgetting they are in presentation mode, and inadvertently sent a private message to another participant being rude about a fellow attendee.

▶ There has been much discussion on the subject of what to wear for a call. It is entirely up to you. You may opt for a smart outfit or decide on a more casual look. But it should go without saying that if you are wearing a smart shirt but sitting in your underwear, you mustn't stand up while the camera's on. If you are self-conscious, it is OK to have the video on for the introduction and then switch off.

▶ Ensure you join the call two or three minutes early and encourage everyone else to do so. Start the call on time, even if you're still waiting for some participants to join the conference.

▶ When you're not talking, mute yourself to avoid distracting background noises (a neighbour will often oblige when you are on a call by using a noisy drill or mowing the lawn).

Synchronous vs. Asynchronous Communication

According to the *Harvard Business Review* article 'Collaborative Overload',[2] the time employees spend on collaboration has increased by 50 per cent over the past two decades. Researchers found it was not uncommon for workers to spend a full 80 per cent of their workdays communicating with colleagues by email (on which workers spend an average of six hours a day); in meetings (which fill up 15 per cent of a company's time, on average); and more recently using instant messaging apps (according to the *Evening Standard*, the average Slack user sends an average of 250 messages a day.[3] We have noted that 1,000-message power users are 'not the exception').[4] So how do you cope with the influx of messages received? A good approach is to make sure the team understands what time frame is reasonable for a response, and that an effort is made to answer the questions or provide the information requested. For example, the team could agree a response time of twenty-four hours. It is best practice to set up a group on a messaging app, such as WhatsApp, for emergencies, and it might be worth pointing out that most of the instant communication platforms have a snooze setting that reminds you of messages.

This method relies on synchronous communication when multiple parties are communicating at the same time, such as in a meeting room or in a face-to-face conversation, and answers are provided or actions taken immediately. This style of communication trickles down into the organization and leads to a culture of 'always on' immediacy to communication when it is not always necessary. This constant messaging or meeting culture results in workers having little time to engage in meaningful, productive work that requires deep concentration.

Before we jump into the detail, let's explore the difference between synchronous and asynchronous communication:

- Synchronous communication is defined as simultaneous communication with all parties being present.

- Asynchronous is a form of communication where an answer or a discussion is not immediate but can emerge over a period of time.

It's important to get the right balance of synchronous and asynchronous communication. A useful tool when deciding which to use is the Eisenhower Decision Principle, which will help you organize your day and ensure you stay focused. Following its rules, agree within the team on a system to indicate which category each message or task falls into. This might be as simple as a labelling convention or having two separate channels in Slack, one for urgent and one for non-urgent, and within those channels giving an indication of whether something is important or not.

| Figure 1: Eisenhower Decision Principle

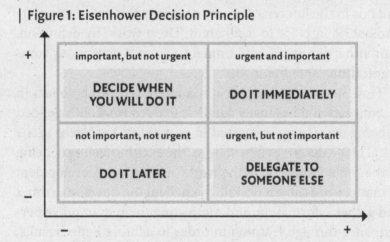

With a clear understanding within the team of what is urgent and what is important, individuals will feel less pressure to respond immediately to everything and there will be no expectation of a reply unless something is both important and urgent. The term for reactive communication is 'shallow work'. It might be tempting to look at an individual's messaging account and measure how many, and how often, messages are sent as an indication of communication, as a basis for meaningful metrics and comparison among your team. There is a trap with collecting messaging metrics, though, and that is to confuse activity with productivity. And indeed, a high volume of messages could be an indicator either of poor communication through misunderstanding, or worse, that the individual is distracting others. Where asynchronous communication brings the biggest benefits is in facilitating the allocation of longer periods of deep work. The term 'deep work' was coined by Georgetown University computer science professor and author Cal Newport and refers to the ability to focus without distraction on a cognitively demanding task.[5] Deep work is the engine of a company and it is in the interests of every company that the right environment be in place to facilitate it. Deep work, by definition, cannot happen in an environment where synchronous communication is predominant.

'Flow state' is a concept that has interested psychologists in recent years and has many parallels to deep work. It is defined as being completely immersed in an activity. Joe Neely, in the Toggl blog,[6] describes flow state as 'the exciting feeling of being in the zone'. Flow state in the workplace leads to development or mastery of a subject or skill, by challenging a person to think and gather information, and motivating them to improve performance through learning in order to achieve better results. Flow state is mostly relevant for creative and technical work that requires a lot of concentration.[7]

The focus on deep work, flow state and asynchronous communication alone does not make the company instantly more productive. The main challenge is finding the right balance and facilitating the deep work, but not to the exclusion of synchronous communication. How can we achieve the perfect balance? Not all teams require as much time for deep work: sales and marketing have different needs from those of a graphic designer, so it would make sense to work on a model for each department. To recognize the need for synchronous communication, one solution is to bring the remote team together for a day of synchronous meetings, or at least schedule a block of time to facilitate this. By structuring these events it becomes easier for the teams to manage their time and save the discussions

| Examples of shallow and deep work:[8]

Examples of Shallow Work	Examples of Deep Work
Processing the emails in your inbox	Drafting a launch plan for a new feature
Responding to colleagues on team chat tools like Slack	Programming
Making phone calls to arrange logistics	Preparing for an upcoming keynote presentation
Attending status update meetings	Researching information on a specific problem

for the allocated time for meetings. For a good check whether you have the balance right, look at your calendar. If it is full of meetings, then you are not being productive at all.

It is helpful to have some guidelines for everyone on what is best practice around synchronous and asynchronous communication, in which the synchronous should be boxed where possible and spontaneous synchronous communication minimized for the truly urgent and important.

Use synchronous communication:

- to build relationships with people in settings such as a team or a one-to-one meeting

- when you need to provide critical feedback or discuss sensitive topics

- when topics are less defined and there are many unknowns, and you need to brainstorm different ideas and explore various solutions

Figure 2: Synchronous and Asynchronous Communication[9]

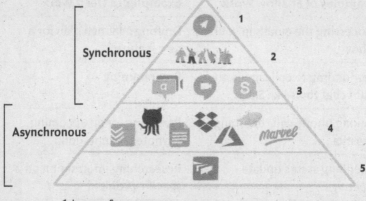

Synchronous

Asynchronous

1. In case of emergency
2. Annual company-wide retreat, experiments with smaller team retreats, and conference
3. Monthly 1:1s, team meetings, ad hoc meetings to discuss particularly complex issues
4. In-context comments on design, copy, code, specs, tasks, etc.
5. Our virtual hub for announcements, ideas, inspiration, feedback, updates, just goofing around, and everything in between

- to bring everyone together and achieve consensus when there is uncertainty or several different views

- to introduce new ideas or projects where there are likely to be many questions

- in an emergency or a crisis that requires immediate attention, such as a key service being unavailable. Notifications for this type of event come through the emergency group on WhatsApp, Telegram or Messenger.

Use asynchronous communication:

- when deep thinking or a flow state is called for, such as research, strategy or project work

- if the person has set time aside for project work, such as coding, design work and analysis

- for less urgent but important work, such as feedback and reviews

- for creating content with no calls to action, such as the quarterly bulletins, financial summaries, curated news articles or image boards.

Asynchronous communication best practice

- Develop a communication guide, either as a simple document or in a frequently-asked-questions format, setting out the channels available and what they should be used for. This guide is a key onboarding document. It is driven by the team leadership or management, who ensure the team follow its stipulations.

- Messages must be precise, direct and have clear expectations. Avoid short messages without context.

- Set expectations on how quickly messages need to be responded to, introduce the channels and labels where appropriate.

- Managers must lead by example, intervene when appropriate and reinforce the asynchronous culture.

- Make it acceptable to use the settings for snooze and busy or unavailable status on the communication channels.

- Encourage the organizers of meetings to involve only those people who are needed and expected to contribute. Use recordings or minutes for information sharing.

Organize effective communication, whether synchronous or asynchronous, and create a structure where everyone understands what is expected:

- Write things down. Make short notes and share.

- Stick to one channel. Information is quickly lost if spread over multiple chat channels, chat applications and emails.

- When setting up groups in the chat channels make sure they are clearly described, and include only those who need to be there. Don't be afraid to archive groups that are no longer relevant. It keeps the chat application manageable.

- Use groups rather than direct messaging in the chat applications to make sure knowledge or conversations are shared. It gives context to discussions.

- Use emojis in chat to show you have read something or found something helpful.

- Pick up the phone or use the video-calling software if you find yourself typing paragraphs into a chat channel.

- Prepare useful information, tell everyone where it is kept and make sure it stays current.

To conclude, asynchronous communication improves productivity by facilitating deep work. Because it is written and shared in public channels, it creates context around discussions and decisions made. It is also invaluable for the onboarding of new team members as it provides a useful repository of the conversations that have taken place.

3 How We Meet

The workplace is where we meet, collaborate, create and communicate. It is not only in the formal settings of meetings, workshops or company presentations but through countless impromptu interactions like sharing a lift, meeting at a coffee station, eating lunch together or joining after work events that we become inspired, create networks and build relationships. These encounters provide us with opportunities to increase our visibility within the company and develop our careers. It's also how we find out what everyone else is up to, usually in the form of a good gossip!

In a remote working context these opportunities are not as immediately obvious, but they do exist; we simply have to be a bit more deliberate about making sure we find them. This section will provide you with the inspiration and practical ideas you need to keep reaping the benefits of meeting in real life, remotely.

Virtual coffee breaks

Chance encounters with colleagues over the coffee machine are a perk of working in the office; they provide opportunities to unwind, build relationships and get to know new colleagues in an informal setting. But that doesn't mean you can't re-create them virtually, though it may feel a little less impromptu to start with.

QUICK TIP

Create a Coffee Break channel in your favourite company messaging app and when someone wants a ten-minute break, grab a coffee and post in the channel 'coffee time' or something with a video link. Anyone who is around and feels like a break joins in.

If spontaneity isn't working, then the other option is to create a recurring slot, say one in the morning and one in the afternoon. People are reminded of the break and everyone who is free can drop in for a chat.

Virtual 'lunch and learn'

In the office it is common to have a lunchtime session when food is provided and there is a speaker, either someone in-house or an external, to give a talk on a given subject and follow up with an informal question and answer session afterwards. This can easily be reproduced virtually with lunch arranged beforehand using a delivery service.

Community or club events

The Covid-19 lockdowns gave rise to a number of online events, such as food-, wine- or beer-tasting where people ordered online and got together on a video call for a tasting session.

Some sports activities are also possible using group apps, such as Strava, where people share their activities, such as running or cycling, and it creates leader boards.

A good way to bring teams together is to hold a quiz night. It can be as simple as finding a quiz on YouTube and self-scoring, or using Zoom and sending the answers to the quiz master on the messaging app. Team interactions develop relationships between team members and some healthy competition between teams brings each team's members together. For a nice tool to assemble an interactive quiz try Mentimeter[1] or Kahoot![2] which support timed questions and have instant results.

Another good initiative is to have a monthly meeting on female leadership, where all the women in the company can discuss the challenges they face in search of recognition and promotion and share useful tips and relevant information.

The real thing

A very effective way to cement working relationships is to physically bring the teams together periodically. While it is possible to work for years with someone and be in frequent contact with video calls, there is no substitute for meeting in person. It is good for new starters to meet the other people in the team and create the social bonds that will enable effective communication. Remotehub.io,[3] the remote hiring website, lists 106 remote companies that organize annual retreats for their staff.

Publishing an agenda for such an event – and sticking to the schedule – may seem a bit rigid, but in order for the get-together to be successful the aims should be clear to all attendees. The experience of a well organized event that accomplishes all its goals reinforces the value of the events; conversely, a poorly prepared and organized event will lead to attendance dropping at future events.

As with any corporate or start-up away day, the schedule could include workshops with brainstorming sessions on shaping the next quarter, some training or coaching or team-building activities. A training day or a workshop is a great way to bring the remote team together in a shared learning experience and also provides opportunities to socialize during the breaks, at lunch or after the event has ended.

Brainstorming sessions are a great opportunity to bring together people from different teams, for example a combination of the sales team, the web developers and the graphic designers. Not only can it help to solve problems but it can aid the building of deeper ties across the company as people get to know each other socially.

Another type of team-building event involves creating shared experiences or inspiration days. This could be an outing to a special place of natural beauty or majestic architecture, or to listen to a lecture by a well-known expert. For remote teams the social setting provides an opportunity to build personal relationships and the shared experience becomes a good talking point.

Company away days

A US company with over 1,000 employees organizes two meetings a year for its staff. One is for the whole company, the other for the individual teams, and at both of them the management team share company information and encourage Q&A sessions.

The general meetup is an event in which the whole company gets together for a couple of days in the same location for fun activities. The smaller meetup consists of a week of various classes and training, together with activities revolving around team bonding. For example, the seating arrangements for meals are worked out beforehand so that team members sit next to different people at each meal and get to talk to many of their colleagues.

These meetups were particularly beneficial for new team members, who say that their integration and work–life balance improved and they felt energized to return home to work on all the things discussed.

With a bit of creativity, we can adapt the remote setting to meet virtually and build stronger social bonds with our colleagues, customers and suppliers.

Where we work

In the traditional world, there was a place of work, and occasionally people worked from home. Remote working has changed all this, and we now have a choice of working from home, co-working spaces and even co-living options. It is important to distinguish a co-working space from a coffee bar that offers free WiFi. Co-working spaces provide the right infrastructure for working but also the essential social element of interacting and creating bonds with people. They are also places to work with fewer distractions than at home, where there can be a temptation to do some households jobs, such as putting the washing machine on or hanging the washing up, or to work with the TV in the background.

Co-working spaces as communities

Just as it is important to develop a remote team as a community, it is also important for the individuals to be involved in their local communities. These secondary communities are found in co-working places, where people contact and interact with others, thus mitigating the potential issues around isolation.

Getting ready, walking or cycling to a local co-working centre brings many benefits for a remote worker.

Firstly, it signifies the break from home to the place of work, and this separation is very important to create boundaries around the working day. We can all picture a remote worker in a T-shirt and pants in their tiny makeshift office with no windows, not going out for days. Secondly, walking or cycling will get the circulation moving and prepare you for a day at the co-working space.

Co-working spaces create communities, as there are opportunities to gather around a coffee machine and strike up conversations or take part in events that are organized by the co-working centre. This can bring interesting perspectives that complement the job. If the people in the co-working centre work in a similar industry, there may be common problems that can be shared, or it can lead to business partnerships.

There are many co-working spaces across towns and cities, and it pays to do some research as they attract different people. For example, designers may cluster in one co-working space whereas software engineers will prefer another. There are also some co-working spaces that market themselves to a particular audience, such as Crypto Plaza[4] in Madrid, Full Node[5] in Berlin or Chainwork[6] in Zurich, aimed at blockchain companies.

It is interesting to compare a co-working space with a centralized office. Often, co-working spaces have private offices for small teams and these are pitched at the start-ups. This could work for a company with remote workers in the same location to gather them in one office. The centralized office is a different beast, even if set up as a 'smart office'. There is a need for meeting rooms and collaboration spaces as well as the normal requirement for office or workspaces. To some extent this is mirrored in co-working spaces, where meeting rooms are available for hire as needed and the different zones (some have comfy chairs grouped for people to meet informally) enable similar interactions. The big difference is the remote worker in a co-working centre will have connections with colleagues in various physical locations and the daily interactions are with people outside their work setting or non-work colleagues.

Co-working space – a centre for a remote community to grow

There are good, bad and indifferent co-working spaces. Even a bad one is probably better than none, as it helps with the separation of work and home life, reduces the 'always on' and creates boundaries around the working day. Above all, it introduces the socialization that comes with work.

The layout and architecture are important. Too many bare walls and hard surfaces make them very noisy, and banks of trestle tables with seats too close together will often result in people wearing headphones to block out the noise, or all the phone booths and informal meeting spaces being blocked. That said, there are many thoughtfully laid out co-working spaces where the trips to the coffee area are conducive to striking up a conversation.

Co-working spaces will often have events, such as talks or social gatherings for members, and this helps foster a community of like-minded people who are either running small or micro businesses or, indeed increasingly, are remote workers.

If you have a choice of co-working spaces, find the right one for you. It is important to the remote worker to combat isolation, and being engaged in a community of like-minded people can bring opportunities or simply friendship.

Co-living and co-working

The co-living movement and co-working go hand in hand, offering the digital nomad a good opportunity to meet, live with and work alongside other digital nomads. Increasingly, the co-living spaces are also used as venues for company retreats, as they are set up to accommodate people and have ready-made workplaces.

Co-living can be seen as a productive environment in which to mix with entrepreneurs and creative individuals and find inspiration from the diverse set of people you meet.

The combination of co-living and co-working makes life much simpler as the alternative is to find accommodation, say through Airbnb, and then figure out where the co-working spaces are. There are, of course, many websites that guide you through this process with comprehensive lists and reviews, but combining co-living and co-working saves hours of research so you can get on more quickly with your business.

New technologies reshaping the way we work

Since the industrial era that led to mass migrations, many new breakthrough technologies have come to light, mainly broadband internet, cloud computing, the personal laptop, the mobile phone and the video call. Having all five elements widely available at low cost has allowed work to be detached from a central place and has expanded where, when and how we work. In the early 2000s, broadband internet made home connections substantially faster, and, in 2003, Skype was released, enabling cheap audio communication for everyone. In 2004, conference-call capabilities were added to the software, and two years after, video conferencing. By 2017, Skype had been downloaded half a billion times. Stanford University professor Nicholas Bloom, whose research focuses on the measurement of management practices and productivity, states that since the release of Skype and for the past fifteen years we could have effectively worked from home but social norms held us back.[7]

The main benefit, though, is to be able to slot easily into a community. The co-working environment is already geared around community, but co-living takes it to the next level.

Co-living is perhaps best for shorter-term arrangements because, while providing the perfect infrastructure and a community of like-minded people, it may lead to living in a bubble of digital nomads and not really engaging with the wider community or seeing different perspectives on life.

What technology do we need?

Three key tech elements are required by remote teams: data security, which is more important than ever; the equipment to make remote working successful; and the tech in the workplace to work with remote teams.

Data security

Data security is often raised as an objection against working remotely and it is important that it is taken seriously. An employee is just as vulnerable to a phishing attack based on social engineering whether in a central office or working remotely. The tools to detect phishing are the same in both situations and so is the security training. Many applications are moving to the cloud as SaaS products, and the challenges posed by the hacking of networks and sophisticated phishing attacks are a threat to all knowledge workers regardless of their location. Either you or your security officer need to ensure that all staff, whether they are seasoned hands or new joiners, are aware of the risks and how to report them. For example, a phishing attack can be simulated to test staff, using tools to create a convincing email with a fake link. Reports will then show who clicked on the link and whether they entered sensitive information (user name and password). The results of the simulation can be anonymized and circulated to show how many people clicked on the links, and to increase awareness that everyone is vulnerable.

It is good practice to equip the remote worker with a laptop which is locked down and managed with restricted administration rights. By hardening the equipment, the first line of defence is put in place. This is then backed up by using a Virtual Private Network (VPN), where a company has the infrastructure, and importantly policies are developed around data security. If a remote worker provides their own equipment, then as a company you have no idea how often the relevant security patches are being supplied, what firewalls, when the last scan was done on the hard drive and what other applications are running (and how vulnerable they are to viruses or malware).

Having just a password to secure an account is less secure than using 2 Factor Authentication (2-FA). The 2-FA gives a second line of protection as it ensures the person logging in has another independent means of authentication. Care should be taken with 2-FA as there are several ways to do this, with an authentication application such as Microsoft or Google Authenticator being more secure than the use of text messages sent with codes which the person then keys in to verify that they have received them.[8]

The policies are important as they cover the basics such as security policies and what can be worked on in a public place such as a co-working centre (it wouldn't be clever to do payroll in a café where anyone can see the screen, or conduct a confidential call on a train).

As with traditional workplace security training, it is just as important for remote workers to understand the tools needed to keep them safe and increasingly how to guard against an ever greater volume of highly plausible emails or fake voice messages purporting to be from the CEO.[9]

During our research interviewing people in larger companies about data security and remote working, a person working in a Fortune 500 global company gave us some insight on how their company managed data security.

The company policy on security and client information is taken very seriously and strong training investment was put in when the team went remote. For all their employees, they instituted compulsory monthly training that is accessed through the company portal. Daily reminders were sent of the security measures that were put in place. To ensure that all the staff were following the rules, the data security team sent out phishing emails to test the employees, who were expected to report these emails and were sent a follow-up email when they did so. If they failed to report the phishing emails, they were asked to undertake further security training. When it comes to client data, this company takes its security seriously.

This practice of phishing tests has also been observed in the banks and even some FinTech companies.

Caution should be taken with social media such as LinkedIn, which can show the location of remote workers; it may not be a good idea to broadcast this.

The remote setup

The best setup for remote working is a combination of technology and services:

- A fast internet connection is vital for communication. There is nothing worse in a video call than the screen freezing or your voice breaking up.

- A quality camera, microphone and headphones.

- A screen and keyboard, better than hunching up over a laptop.

- A video-calling subscription. It is a false economy to use the 'free' video services, such as Skype or Hangouts, as some of them have restrictions. For example, Zoom allow only up to forty minutes for a group call, and whereby.com restrict a call to four people. The paid services, such as Zoom, Microsoft Teams or the G-Suite version of Hangouts, have the quality needed for business calls and are a prerequisite for connecting remote teams.

- Messaging apps. A must for asynchronous communication, discussed earlier. Groups on messaging apps can quickly get out of hand, so it helps to have someone responsible for managing and updating the groups. It is also best practice to set up some boundaries. For example, it is good to leave an emoji to indicate someone has been helpful, and to suggest in the guidance notes which one (the beer emoji might not always be an appropriate choice).

- Cloud storage. Documents must be stored in a central system that is quickly accessible to everyone on the team.

Sharepoint, G-Drive and other cloud-based software can be powerful tools for the remote manager.

- Remote whiteboards. Cloud-based whiteboards cater to the needs of remote teams or enterprise teams working across several geographic locations, allowing them to collaborate online using virtual tools, which can be used asynchronously. A session by team members clustered around one time zone can then be picked up by a further cluster in a different time zone.

- Expenses management system. A centralized and automated place to process invoices and to approve and manage the spending of the remote teams whether on company cards or as refundable out-of-pocket expenses.

CASE STUDY

Yusef's remote toolbox

Yusef leads the design team of five people spread across a few locations and has been with the company for five years, making him a veteran remote worker.

Yusef has two machines, one for home and one for work. He uses his home laptop to browse the net, stream films and for the odd app. He has loaded Spotify so he can listen to music as a way of helping him concentrate.

His work machine is a meaty laptop that has a good video card, and he has invested in a comfortable headset with a cardioid mic he can use for the conference calls. He has a bag with a charger (and various converters), a power bank, a USB stick and a gadget that converts USB into an ethernet port (and a cable).

Yusef has Slack, Figma, Photoshop, Dropbox, Zoom and the company G-Suite account. There are a bunch of cloud apps he uses for time entry, the HR system and the stock picture library.

Having a work machine keeps Yusef focused on work, and the apps support his remote job and enable him to do it productively.

The tech toolkit for the workplace

Once the remote team have the best setup with the best laptop, camera, microphone and a speedy data connection, we also must consider what the workplace team need because many companies employ a hybrid model with both remote workers and people in the workplace.

On the assumption that people will spend some time in the workplace and some time working remotely, then they will be using the same laptop in both locations and have the headsets they need for video calls.

Each person should be given the option to use a screen and keyboard at their desk, whether they are dedicated or hot desks, as they enjoy in the remote place (home or co-working space).

There must be adequate provision of meeting rooms with video and a good system of microphones and speakers. Pay particular attention to the combined microphone and speakers, such as those made by Jabra[10] or Logitec,[11] as this makes the difference between being heard clearly and engaging with the remote team or not.

Without this or in the absence of meeting rooms people will join calls at their desks, which potentially causes issues in an open plan office or, worse, will join the calls on their mobiles to get away from their desks and sit somewhere noisy like a coffee bar or the canteen.

The setup of remote first, by which we mean the technology, has to be in place to facilitate the remote team, ensure it stays well connected and can work productively.

The technology to enable teams to work together remotely is here and accessible to all, there is no doubt about that. In this section, we went over the different measures to consider in order to ensure that communication and collaboration happen smoothly in distributed teams. This alone, however, does not guarantee success; you also require good governance. In the next section we will discuss the various managerial challenges of maintaining high productivity, increasing team collaboration and information sharing.

Part 2   Managing a Remote Team

4 Office-based vs. Remote

What makes you an effective remote manager? Just like in the office, you'll need to get the best work from your team; you will set objectives, organize progress reports, help resolve issues and report the team's achievements. In a remote setting, you have the added benefit of working innovatively; you can break the mould and try new things as you are freed from the traditions of the office setting. For example, you can bring in tracking of objectives rather than valuing how long people spend at their desks, and you can focus on what matters rather than being distracted by the characters in the office that shout the loudest. As a remote manager, you'll develop skills in areas such as setting and managing key objectives and results, which will make your team more effective than just relying on instinct. In this section we help guide you through making the most of managing a remote team.

Here's a look at the key differences between office-based managing and remote managing:

Office-based manager	Remote manager
9–5 hours: your team will likely work on a similar clock, you'll see them at their desks or attending meetings.	**Flexibility:** your team can work when it suits them best. You'll need to develop trust and empower your team to organize their time.
Presenteeism: an employee's value may be measured against their hours clocked and visibility within the office.	**Goal-based assessment:** remote working allows managers to focus on outcomesrather than hours clocked.
Hierarchical structure: the traditional office tends to favour a chain of command.	**Flat structure:** each employee should be responsible for their own work and rsponsible for decisions made.
Face-to-face communication: employees may be motivated by receiving public praise for good work.	**Remote communication:** make time to celebrate success and bring it to the attention of the rest of the team.
Visibility: your employees will likely work near you and can ask for help at any time.	**Virtual reality:** schedule regular catch-ups with team members and keep your calendar up to date so it's clear when they can get in touch.

5 Collaboration and Communication

The five conversations

Gallup workplace research, titled 'How to Manage the Loneliness and Isolation of Remote Workers',[1] recommends frequent and ongoing conversations between managers and their remote teams. A wide-ranging spectrum of conversations from serious to more informal should aim to inspire innovation to help the team and organization thrive, increase engagement and motivation of team members and avoid team members feeling isolated.

The Gallup research listed five types of manager–subordinate conversations:

- quick connect
- check-in
- developmental coaching
- progress review
- role and relationship development

The five types drive performance. To achieve results, these different types of conversations must be engaged in regularly and questions must be dealt with properly: direct questions get direct answers. These conversations are oriented towards engagement and keeping managers focused, fostering their understanding of their remote employees by considering their unique contributions, witnessing how they communicate and noticing how they respond to workplace situations.

What did you work on today?

A very helpful practice Basecamp have in place is the automatic question at the end of every workday: 'What did you work on today?'[2] All answers are shared with everyone in the company, displayed in a single page and grouped by date, so that anyone who would like to know what is going on in the company can do so by accessing this document. Basecamp see this routine as a good exercise for team members to reflect on their work and put in perspective everyone's accountability in the company. They also apply the same method on a weekly review and add optional social questions such as 'What book are you reading?' or 'What are you doing this weekend?'

Your communication toolkit

There are several communication tools important for remote teams. The main chat applications, such as Slack, Teams, Hangouts or Discord, are similar in terms of features, the ability to create both public and private groups, video calling and direct messaging. The most important criterion when creating groups is to give them meaningful names in order to prevent situations arising when the whole company is chatting all day long in the same channel, making it impossible to follow who is talking about what and to whom. It is also good to encourage people to chat in groups rather than direct messages, so that information is shared. If possible, connect the video-calling application so it is easy to call someone rather than type long essays back and forth.

The use of emojis is a minefield as not all generations are fluent in 'emoji'; a simple guide might be helpful and beneficial. Using emojis allows team members' personalities to shine through, shows empathy and spreads positivity. It can encourage people to mark a post as useful (you should specify which emoji to use). At its simplest, a thumbs-up shows you have read something. Dr Banerjee[3], at the University of Chichester, encourages the use of emojis to fill the gap of the non-verbal cues, as they act *as a proxy cue of attitude of the communicator*. So don't be afraid to add the odd smiley face, thumbs-up or round of applause emoji to the end of your message. Nowadays any company can create custom emojis and such personal features can result in closer bonds between team members and build friendlier work relationships.

Tips for the use of emojis in business communication:

- Stick with the basic emojis and, most importantly, the ones that have a general meaning.

- Safe to use at work: 🔒 🖼 📳☺ 😎 🐾 🦍 💡 ☑ ✚ ❎ 📷

- Avoid at work: 💩 🥊 🫦 💧 😬 🐮 👅 😶 👾[4]

- Avoid softening a hard message with a smiley or other emoji as it may come across as a passive-aggressive message.

- Emojis work best when they are accompanied by a written message; use them to reinforce the true intent of a message, not to communicate a new one.

6 Hybrid Teams

Hybrid teams, those which combine office-based workers and remote workers, are becoming more common as companies move to accommodate social distancing and flexible working. A hybrid team can be one of the biggest challenges you come up against when managing a remote team, and you'll need to create practices to ensure all employees are in sync.

Trello[1] believe that to succeed in building hybrid teams, you must ensure that you have 'a corporate culture and work environment where collaboration can thrive from anywhere'. The key to this is talking with your team about how you can best work together. Discuss when and how you'll communicate, and stipulate that all team meetings will be online, as hybrid meetings are unfair to those physically not in the space. Set some rules for meetings: questions to be asked in the chat channels and read out by the person in charge of the meeting, and plenty of opportunity allowed for everyone who wants to contribute to answer the questions. You need an eagle eye to spot cliques forming within your team, especially if there are divisions between the onsite and the remote people. It is all too easy for a group, usually in the workplace, to have lunch together or socialize after work and naturally forget their remote working colleagues. Clearly you cannot stop people socializing, but you must ensure that discussions, information provided and decisions made at meetings are fully documented so that everyone knows what is going on.

One good way of connecting two teams is to have a buddy system where one remote person is teamed up with an onsite person. Not only does it ensure the remote person is plugged into what is going on in the office but it means there is someone to whom they can send a quick message, for example to find out if someone in the office is at their desk.

You must ensure that the onsite people use the chat channels to include the remote people where possible. If there are discussions held in person, someone must be assigned to write up the notes of the conversation, especially when actions are decided upon and deadlines are set. These notes should be put in a shared folder that everyone has access to.

One of the issues that hybrid teams experience is the fact that there are more distractions in the office and people feel more productive in a remote environment. This must be considered, especially if there are team members who spend most of their time in the workplace as this will impact the amount of deep work they do. Ensure that a person in this situation is encouraged to do the deep work when working remotely, or that they can reserve a space in the calendar to focus on the deep work without distractions.

QUICK TIPS

▶ For those in the office: use a conference room rather than all huddle around separate laptops.

▶ If there are multiple laptops connected, be mindful of muting microphones to avoid echo.

▶ Assign someone to type questions into the chat channels and read out any that come in so that everyone is clear about what is being discussed.

▶ The meeting chair should pause the meeting from time to time to encourage participation by the remote workers and ask if they have any questions or comments to add.

7 Creating a Virtual Safe Space

Just like in real life, creating virtual safe spaces is crucial for the wellness of all employees. Virtual meetings can be tricky because they diminish the ability to see facial expressions or social cues that might be obvious during in-person meetings. Setting some ground rules will make all work gatherings, from chat channels to meetings, safe spaces for all.

1. Make small talk inclusive: be aware that some topics of conversation might be exclusive to members of the team of a particular class, gender, race or sexuality. For example, discussing expensive holidays or restaurants might make some less privileged colleagues feel excluded.

2. Monitor chat spaces for language that might exclude certain employees.

3. Create a code word that will be used to highlight any non-inclusive language or behaviour during meetings.

4. Create an equal playing field: ensure the meeting chair is conscious of anyone talking over others. Everyone in the team should feel free to express their views regardless of their level of seniority.

To make things clear and unambiguous it is important that the team understands why things are done they way they are.

- Effective communication is of utmost importance: creating a safe space will ensure everyone feels valued and respected and able to do their best work

- If someone asks a question in private, make the reply public, as it is likely that others will have the same question.

- Celebrate and recognize when tasks or milestones are achieved.

- Cultivate the practice of sharing questions, answers, doubts, announcements and successes through open channels.

- Remember to send periodic updates by email. Daily is too frequent, as it veers towards micromanagement; monthly is not frequent enough, as the team might feel abandoned.

- Invest time and money in project management tools that give teams visibility on what they are doing and how it affects the work of others and the company as a whole. Implementing these tools can be resource-consuming, so make your choice well and make sure everyone is comfortable with it.

Since the company's inception, distributed teams have been in the DNA of ifeel, an online therapy platform. They have invested a lot of time and money into finding the most suitable project management tool. They tried several tools until they found the one that worked best for their needs and could be integrated with the other tools they use internally. The tool chosen allowed information to be centralized. Each project and task has an assigned owner and the open tickets are updated. Martin Villanueva Ordás, co-founder and COO of ifeel, did confess that is was very time consuming to set it up, but he added that work had never been so cohesive, agile and transparent as since it had all been put in place.

8 Outcomes-driven Management

The key to highly effective teams is creating a delivery or execution mindset. This approach focuses individuals and teams on a concrete result, not the process required to achieve it. Employees then have a high degree of autonomy to use their own unique talents to reach goals in their own way. The opposite approach – a command-and-control style of management – forces managers to police their employees. This is not advisable for a whole host of reasons, but it's also impossible in a remote setting. Instead, by focusing on outcomes, you can allow your team freedom and control over their time, but it also facilitates accountability for their outcomes and responsibility for the achievement of their set goals.

In an office setting it is easy to have the dashboards on a big screen, running with graphics showing the progress of the project and how much code has been cut, or the sales metrics of how many new leads have been generated, the number of deals closed and the progress of the monthly targets. Being able to see and share these metrics gives people a sense of purpose, but it presents a challenge in a remote setting. The most effective way to share this information is to have it readily available to all staff and to use the communication channels to draw people to the dashboards with messages such as 'almost there on the sales targets and 10 days to do before month-end' with a link. There are dashboards for goal tracking and status reporting, such as weekdone.com[1] or Hubspot's[2] dashboards for sales figures.

Implementing a results-driven style of working:

- Get everyone on the same page by communicating direction and strategy to build rapport with team members and increase engagement for those who feel lost.

- Empower team members through motivation and inspiration to achieve high performance and strong work ethic.

- Foster more open channels of communication for stronger sense of collaboration and teamwork.

- Set stretch goals to push for success, achievement and continuous learning. Collect feedback and utilize the data to improve either the processes or organizational culture nuances.

9 Goal Setting and Accountability

An aligned team is one that aspires to achieve the same vision, understands the goals and is made up of individuals who know how to contribute their strengths to the team. Team alignment becomes even more important when you work remotely or as a hybrid. As a manager, how do you make sure each team member is aligned and understands what success looks like for their team?

- Reflect on previous goals to determine the new goals: were they ambitious enough? What was done well? What was learned from the challenges the team went through?

- Results must be measurable and numerical; ensure they are achievable with a workload that is healthy.

- Make your team be accountable for their work and take ownership.

- Discuss the new goals via video call, first individually and then in a team meeting – expectations must be well communicated and clear to all.

- Follow up and provide updates on the progress of the goal; break the goal into different milestones to be achieved.

- Identify skills development and improvement so that managers can support team members in reaching their full potential.

Accountability

Accountability is defined as the responsibility of every individual to complete the task they have been assigned. To make this work in a remote setting, there must be clear reporting structures, goals and meetings (video calls and screen sharing to foster close collaboration), and the key part is to make sure that there is a person accountable for each task or project. Trust is a fundamental necessity in the success and high functioning of a remote team and accountability fosters trust. ReCharge, the remote first company with over 250 employees across multiple continents,[1] encourage people to have task lists and tick them off to help define the projects they are accountable for. These task lists must be scheduled and have a certain time frame associated with them. If they are open ended, the responsibility for completing them is absent, thus there is no accountability.

Constructive accountability

Constructive accountability, when applied by the manager, broadens and builds the strengths of the team by moving accountability into everyday work. J.G. Seiling,[2] in the 2005 paper 'Moving from Individual to Constructive Accountability', defines constructive accountability as an ongoing conversation during the process of work achievements that creates the relationship and pushes for collective responsibilities for each outcome. You know this is going wrong when a blame culture emerges.

Managers should also be mindful of which team members

to involve in team sessions, and at times let the team manage itself. Managers should encourage their teams to discuss and share their opinions on what could be done better, thus fostering a collaborative accountability and creating a cycle of continuous improvement.

Ownership

When it is necessary to make a choice, there must be someone who explains the decision to be made (decision-maker) and someone who will drive the research, decision process and follow through (owner). You need to make sure that you identify the decision-maker and owner and communicate this to your team and any external stakeholders.

The ownership assignation is very important, particularly in documentation. Even if documents are collaborative, each document/folder must have an owner who will be responsible for its quality and maintenance.

From an individual perspective, ownership encourages team members to think and find ways forward. Managers should not be providing all the answers and directions because this leads to dependency, which is non optimal in remote teams as the goal is to minimize the need for constant communication. The 'extreme ownership' concept and technique first introduced by Jocko Willink and Leif Babin in their book *Extreme Ownership: How U.S. Navy SEALs Lead and Win*, in which they explain how communication and self-management are critical in the battlefield, can be replicated perfectly in the remote working model as these two factors are equally important and crucial for remote teams. When applied to a remote setup, the concept requires all team members to 'own' one area of the business or project. For new team members, taking ownership does not mean they are on their own from day one. They will require help, support and time to learn the process. Establishing the ownership mentality will result in better and faster decision-making.

10 Measuring Performance

The most common and proven way to measure performance is either through OKRs (Objectives and Key Results), KPIs (Key Performance Indicators) or CI (Continuous Improvement) techniques. In the following sections, we will examine the three performance management tools.

Effective performance management plans are the key to reducing costs, increasing productivity and providing a well balanced and healthy environment for team members. Managers must be consistent in measuring performance and, most importantly, engage in an ongoing communication process of evaluation and feedback with their team members. Measuring performance requires a little adjustment when teams are remote, and it is very important to set up these tools early on to ensure that the culture of the company is open. In remote working, you cannot always see how someone is doing. In an office, this is a little easier to detect, although it can sometimes be difficult to distinguish between busy and productive, even when you are sitting next to someone.

Objectives and Key Results (OKRs) and Key Performance Indicators (KPIs)

Measuring performance in a more quantitative way can be done using techniques such as setting OKRs and having a clear link of business priorities set to the goals, which in turn determine KPIs. Start by introducing the team's objectives and then divide the team goals into individual ones. The results must be discussed frequently, and it must also be stressed that the business goals are not static and may be realigned from time to time according to opportunities or events in the marketplace. The team must be open to pivoting if required to realign, as agility and resilience are important to the success of a team.

OKR[1] is a new technique used by technology companies, such as Google, who pioneered it. It works as follows: each department must set objectives in line with the company's goals, and set objectives with metrics for each person so that everyone has a role (that can be measurable) which is aligned with the company's main objective. Doerr's formula is the best way to explain the structure of an OKR: *I will (Objective) as measured by (this set of Key Results).* For example, I will improve visitor numbers on the website by optimizing the content as measured by the number of page visits and time spent on the page.

The theory seems very simple and straightforward but putting it in practice requires a lot of effort from the management team. As a tool for a remote team it brings in a good deal of clarity and helps reduce misunderstandings.

Doist struggled to implement OKRs[2] and experimented with Spotify's engineering cultural system,[3] in the end creating a hybrid, DO system, which worked for them. Spotify stopped using OKRs in 2014 once they reached a point where their company priorities and product strategy were aligned. Since then, each area has their two-year goal along with a data-based betting system to know the work the team needs to do.[4]

The best way to set the OKRs varies depending on the stage your company is at. For an early stage company, the vision and company goals must be clear and each team member's goals must relate directly to the company's. Conversely, if the company is already mature and some roles very well defined, another way to set the OKRs is to work from the bottom up.

Kaizen or Continuous Improvement

Introduced by US occupation forces after the Second World War to help rebuild Japanese manufacturing, Kaizen or Continuous Improvement is the mindset of striving for perfection by making many small improvements all the time. A key aspect of CI is to measure and look at the root causes of problems using the 'Five Why' technique (keep asking why until you find the cause).

A 'Five Why' example

Issue to examine: A recent software release has more bugs than was expected.

Why was the release full of bugs?

Why? Because the Quality Assurance team did not have time to finish all the testing.

Why? Because the developers dropped all the code at the last minute.

Why? Because it was all new and done by different teams and only came together at the last minute.

Why? Because the planning did not account for the work being done by different teams.

The root cause was identified, and can be remedied by planning future releases so that the software is incrementally tested through the development cycle.

The continuous improvement mindset of measure, improve, fix and assess quickly highlights any potential issues so they can be addressed before they become big problems. This rapid fixing of small problems to create robust systems is described by Nassim Taleb in his book *Antifragile*.[5]

This iterative improvement process aligns easily with remote teams as it can quickly become part of the daily work routine and needs little organization or lengthy evaluation periods.

Performance management tracking, tools and best practices

There are many new performance management platforms that help to retrieve this information; some are automated or have a cost, others require proper planning to customize them for teams and demand the involvement and time of all stakeholders. For example, using Agile methodologies teams can capture estimates and record actual time spent, so it becomes possible to measure the progress of the project and obtain qualified estimates on its delivery date.

Any tool used must be clearly presented to the team by

explaining its purpose and the desired outcome and ensuring that the whole team participates. The results collected must be discussed among the managers and positive change must come out of it. Many companies have the right intentions but tend to fail at implementing them and making use of this information positively.

The soft skills you need in a remote setting are similar to those you need in the office. Firstly, avoiding blame is paramount as this discourages transparency and can create an environment where mistakes are hidden. Instead, you must deliver feedback in a constructive way, discussing what went wrong and what can be learned from the experience. It may be necessary to document several actions and follow them up.

Here is an example:

Your team has begun a project for a new client, and are keen to show the client the first version of their designs. However, they get some very negative feedback. You assemble the team to try to figure out where the mismatch of expectations happened. Following a review, it becomes clear that the drafts met the brief. The next step is to talk it through with the sales team, where it becomes apparent that a key piece of information was not uploaded. You call the team together again and explain what happened and they then figure out how to make the changes in light of the missing information. The lesson learned is to check with the sales team that all the information has been captured and uploaded to the project drive. At the next client meeting there is a positive response.

When there are issues, document the points raised and actions agreed, ensure that there is a person who takes ownership, and schedule follow-ups. This signals that you want the team to learn from the problem and will follow the matter up, and that this was not a pointless exercise with no action taken.

There are times when you must be firm and explain to a member of the team where something is not acceptable or that something was done that was not right. For example, if a person left some half-finished work for a colleague to complete just before a deadline, then that person must be told what the expectations are and why the inaction was unacceptable. If the situation arises again with the same person, then you have to consider disciplinary measures.

Just as the feedback discussion with the individual is important, another especially important aspect for you is to build trust. This is not unique to remote managers, but it is heightened by how easy it is to misunderstand communication in a remote setting. Building trust is not one of those things you can do by following five steps you find through a Google search.

You build trust by showing respect for your staff in your actions. For example: don't cancel one-on-one meetings at the last minute (if you do so, you signal that they are not important); help them find answers to things they are blocked on rather than just telling them the answer; ask them questions and guide them so they learn the most; back them up in difficult situations and escalate issues where they feel they have less authority. Above all, be fair and consistent across the team; managers who form cliques rarely have a fully engaged team. Remember that trust is a process that is built over time but can be destroyed very quickly.

It is helpful to avoid the following:

- Cancelling meetings with your direct reports at the last minute

- Giving direct answers to a question (unless they are asking the time); use the situation as a learning opportunity

- Automatically agreeing with the customer or manager rather than your team member

- Favouritism to certain team members. This can be subconscious and being aware of it helps to avoid it.

Alex Turnbull, co-founder and CEO of Groove, a SaaS product that makes it easier for teams to manage customer service, says that one-on-one meetings have saved their company culture.[6] Even though these meetings are time-consuming, the returns pay off as the company grows. Every two weeks, he blocks out eight hours to check in with everyone on his team, a practice he started implementing at a later stage and admits wishing he had begun doing it a lot earlier. During these one-on-ones, he and the team member discuss what they are working on, how they feel about the company and what challenges they foresee it could face.

This practice changed the company culture from one of silos, where everyone was working in their own space aside from Slack and weekly calls, to a more involved culture. As a result of these one-on-ones, communication on Slack increased and became more honest and more opinions were voiced. It also improved team alignment as team members were led to answer the question 'why' for each of their tasks and to understand their role in the bigger picture of the company. Lastly, employee happiness grew as there was now room to discuss unaddressed issues and greater clarity on business activities which in turn resulted in increased retention of team members.

According to Alex Turnbull, demanding feedback and being patient are two important ingredients in creating a successful company culture.

Another useful tool in boosting performance is a mentor scheme. The mentee benefits from practical advice and acquires knowledge, while the mentor can hone their skills to be able to provide instruction. It can be very satisfying to witness a person develop in their role.

A bank in the 1990s was considering introducing a mentor scheme and circulated a short survey to its staff to find out how many people would consider being a mentor and how many thought they would benefit from being mentored. A huge percentage of the responders said they were willing to be mentors but very few asked to be mentored. Before implementing such a scheme, consideration must be given to how to do it successfully. It generally works well with everybody. In a remote setting the support can be very valuable.

A short team survey can establish if there are issues around performance, and these may lead to changes in how a team is organized. A couple of key questions would be: 'Do you get all the information you need in time to execute a client project?' or 'Are the project deadlines realistic to produce outstanding work for our clients?' The Hubstaff blog's suggested questions include: *'Do you enjoy being a member of your team?' (Rate from 1 to 10)* and *'How often do you feel stressed out at work?' (Open answer)*.[7]

Niamh, a programmer at a start-up, London

Niamh is celebrating her first year as a remote manager in a machine-learning start-up and comparing it to her previous job as a manager in a team based in Shoreditch in London.

In her old job the whole team was in one office. Team members had their routines of morning coffee and team meeting, and there were regular whiteboarding sessions in the corner of the office with a barrage of Post-it notes as ideas were written down. She thought that performance management added an overhead that was not needed as she could see what the team was up to and they were delivering.

The new job is Niamh's first remote job as a manager and she has been introduced to the performance management tools and processes, which she has found helpful in identifying areas where some degree of intervention, such as introducing a mentor programme, has enabled knowledge transfer. She has made changes to the team structure to deal with some issues highlighted in staff surveys.

Niamh has a weekly call with each of her team members. She reviews the previous week's objectives and, if they have not been met, she explores the reasons why and discusses what actions should be taken. It might be for Niamh to escalate or intervene if the person is being assigned lots of work by someone else. Then she sets each team member's objectives for the following week.

Niamh has joined a subcommittee to evaluate and monitor the processes around performance measurement to ensure they have the most appropriate practices in place for the company's size and needs.

11   Decision-making

Every success or mishap, every opportunity seized or missed, is the result of a decision that was made or not by someone. Decisions are what governs every business, and in many companies decisions consistently get stuck during the process. High-performing teams make the right decision quickly and effectively and execute these decisions consistently. In a remote environment, it can be very difficult to get everyone together in a meeting to discuss a decision to be made and you cannot rely on face-to-face communication. Therefore a process must be put in place that relies on the same concepts of asynchronous communication and allows a team to take the best decisions together.

Asynchronous decision-making

Asynchronous decision-making is a very efficient way for your team to move forward and take decisions with minimal meetings. It is extensively used in open source projects and it is quite impressive to see how people come together and contribute to a project that has an end goal, without meeting and simply through asynchronous communication. Open source, as defined in the website opensource.guide, means anybody is free to use, modify and distribute a project, thus lowering barriers to collaboration and improvement in decision-making.[1] This method of decision-making requires a lot of planning and begins with the setting up of a process, backed up with a central communication channel with a solid consensus-building mechanism. It is ideal to have one channel to discuss and brainstorm on the topic and another to have a voting poll. In remote setups, requiring unanimity or allowing vetoes in decision-making can block progress, and for this reason they should favour consensus which is defined as the 'widespread agreement among people who have decision power'.[2] Many decision-making packages exist on the market today that assist with the complete collaborative decision-making processes and can be integrated with any communication and project management tool used internally.

A suggested flow would look like this:

- Assign people to a decision that needs to be made.

- Start a discussion thread.

- Write a proposal and create a poll.

- Disclose results and outcomes.

Using asynchronous decision-making strategies, you will see an increase in productivity by promoting collaboration and by making the process more time-efficient. Once a decision has been made, a plan has to be put into action by assigning an owner who is responsible for the delivery of the objectives, for escalating any issues to the decision-maker and for keeping the stakeholders informed.

12 Conflict Resolution

Conflict can arise in remote teams just as it can in any working environment. It cannot be avoided, nor should it be. In many cases it can be a mechanism for growth, and challenging each other on difficult issues is an important part of the checks and balances of any company. In a remote working context, teams should build effective conflict management into how they work and be aware of the process. Ideally, it should be a process developed as part of the company culture, that is known by all members and preferably explained during the onboarding process. Moving it into the normal day-to-day business removes any stigma that might be associated with conflict. As a prevention exercise, it is there to avoid issues escalating and spilling over into personal conflict. A worker feeling able to ask for mediation to resolve an issue is a sign of a healthy company culture. Conflict management in remote work can be smoother than face-to-face since it becomes a documented process that contributes to the fabric of the culture.

The role of the mediator is fundamental, and is usually undertaken by managers or team leaders. A mediator needs to have training as it is too important a role to rely merely on 'good judgement'. It is important to know that a mediator is only as effective as the trust deposited in them by all parties. For mediation to succeed, a key element is establishing a

company culture of trust in which all parties respect the mediator and good channels of communication are in place to enable
the timely resolution of problems.

There are two sources of disagreements, the written and the
spoken.

Written disagreements

Written disagreements often come about in the chat channels
rather than in formal documents. Because of the instantane-
ous nature of chat, responses are not always considered and
there is much room for misinterpretation of meaning or misunderstanding of what is being said. And, while there is a real
benefit in having an unquestionable record of what was 'said'
and when, non-verbal cues are evidently missing. The written
form of communication can lack context or nuance whereas
communication in person allows the parties to ask for clarifica-
tions. In an article in the *New York Times*, Allan and Barbara
Pease revealed that more than 50 per cent of communication
is done non-verbally,[1] which highlights the shortcomings of
chat channels.

Verbal disagreements

Verbal disputes are very real but there is none of the evidence
we see in written disputes, merely the testimony of each party.
These disputes are less common in the remote working setting
as much of the communication is done using chat or email.

Mediation

The first step for anyone caught up in a conflict is to request mediation from their manager or team leader. Sometimes it may be a team leader who asks for mediation and needs to involve their manager.

Mediation aims to bring objectivity to the conflict and remove emotion from the discussion.

Here are the steps in the mediation process:

- The mediator speaks to all the parties involved and produces a written summary of their views of the conflict. It is important that the facts are recorded.

- The mediator sends the documented summary of the conversations to each party for review.

- If it is a written dispute, the mediator gathers the documented conversations and summarizes.

- The parties are invited to a video call, if all are remote, to resolve the dispute. The agenda is well defined in advance and takes the form of the mediator presenting the summary of the conversations, followed by each party having their say. The mediator then works with the parties to achieve closure where possible.

- The outcome of the meeting is sent out in writing.

The mediator has an important role to find a path for the parties involved to meet in the middle and achieve closure. The prime objective is to stop the parties disputing the issue further. How is this done in practice? In resolving a dispute there is often not one single outcome but a set of resolutions that the parties can agree on.

The mediator should work with the participants to achieve:

- an acknowledgement of each party's views

- a commitment to change behaviour

- a commitment to a regular review of the agreement reached

- an agreement to review policies and procedures

- an agreement to share work more fairly and provide greater responsibility.

CASE STUDY

Carmen, Mateo and Kumud

Carmen has some very strong views about a messaging protocol which forms an important part of the new system they are designing; Mateo is adamant that the protocol Carmen is advocating is a disaster waiting to happen.

Their discussion got very heated at the planning meeting and it spilled over into the next meeting. It was clear that Kumud, as team leader, should step in.

Kumud asked them both to come up with the pros and cons of the messaging protocol to try to bring some objectivity to the discussion.

Unfortunately, neither Carmen nor Mateo were willing to cede ground and did not give the process the full commitment that Kumud wanted. He started sensing that matters were close to getting personal.

Kumud invited Carmen and Mateo to a video call, and gave them an agenda before the meeting specifying that each would have five minutes to present their case without the other one interrupting, and at the end of each presentation Kumud would ask questions.

Kumud carefully laid out the arguments that both had expressed and took care to highlight where they were talking about the same thing and where their points differed. This objective approach removed emotion from the discussions and the facts were made clear.

Kumud then summarized and later came to a decision, told them how he had arrived at it and followed up with an email to both with the meeting notes.

The conflict, it turned out, was due to a misunderstanding of how Carmen wanted to use the software, and the fact that Mateo had based his opinion on an older version of the software used in a previous project. Both had made some basic assumptions and it became clear when they were making their case that they had not communicated them, thinking it was obvious. After the analysis from Kumud, Carmen and Mateo re-examined what Carmen was proposing and learnt from Mateo's experience of the issues he had come across in his earlier project. The result was some modifications of the proposal and a few additions both realized were important.

In the case of Carmen and Mateo, Kumud was able to come up with a resolution which involved both parties finding a compromise. Other outcomes could have been for both parties to acknowledge each other's viewpoint and stop arguing, or agree to disagree but to stop discussing the matter.

When a conflict becomes emotional, the discussions must be stopped and the arguments must be objectively documented and summarized. Without emotion, a qualitative decision can be made and both parties should see reason.

Further measures are available, such as arbitration, where the parties agree that the arbiter makes a final decision and that they are bound by the outcome.

13 Happiness at Work

Happiness at work can be equated with job satisfaction, having a sense of purpose, achievement, competence and recognition or respect from your team or others in your industry. Remote working is no different. But remote workers may have a different opinion about what makes a job satisfying. Most people enjoy getting things done to the best of their ability, and being given the responsibility to make decisions and contribute. The difference between an office or centrally based worker and a remote worker is that the office worker usually timeboxes their day to 'normal working' hours, whereas a remote worker may cherish flexible working patterns, such as the ability to manage childcare, or taking a longer lunch break to embrace a warm sunny day. But, whatever motivates your staff, the conclusion is the same: companies with happy employees outperform the competition by 20 per cent.

Here are some steps you can take to create a happy, productive team:

- Consistently deliver praise and recognition; this is best done in the presence of other team members.

- Hold a weekly ten-minute Zoom call to celebrate any successes.

- Create a Slack channel where team members can share things they are proud of.

- Write an impromptu note when you notice someone going above and beyond. You can never underestimate the power that this has in motivating your team.

Make work fulfilling. No one wants to feel that their work doesn't matter. Make sure each employee knows why they are doing what they are doing and the impact their work has. Zappos are a good example. They deliver shoes and clothing but their mission is to 'deliver happiness'. All new hires spend two weeks fielding customer service calls, no matter which department they're going to be working for, so they see the value of their work.

Invest in your team's personal and professional growth. When employees feel they're stagnating, that's when they start looking for something new. Happiness is about growing and expanding your capabilities.

You could:

- Subsidize education and learning resources for your team members who want to take classes, attend conferences or improve their skills on online courses.

- Host 'lunch and learns' where a team member presents a topic he or she is passionate about, or bring in an external speaker.

- Start a book, podcast or film club.

How happy is your team?

There are many platforms on the market offering tools to measure employee happiness that can be integrated with a company's communication tool, such as fridaypulse. com, happyatwork.io and happier.com, to name a few.

Career progression

Remote workers also have goals and aspirations and they deserve the same type of career development frameworks and opportunities as office-based workers. Career progression or career pathing is the process by which managers empower team members to map out different scenarios based on the defined accomplishments and skills needed for a specific position.

Career progression is important for team retention, and managers should encourage their team members to develop their skills and maybe find a path to becoming an expert in their field by investing in training, and encouraging them to publish articles or to speak at events.

Managers should ensure they discuss team members' goals and aspirations and track their progress. It's important to have a dialogue with your team on a regular basis, and you should consider this a specific topic for a video call, or combine it with the quarterly team get-togethers by taking time for each member of the team. One-on-one meetings are a great place to have these discussions. Document the conversations, making a note of the action points, and review the situation at the next session to assess progress or to identify any changes required.

Building a management strategy for career path planning:

- Define success with the team: what is a win?

- Constantly remind everyone of the organization's goal and where they fit into the picture.

- Create short-term goals, long-term goals and a defined process for promotion.

- Regularly check in with the team and keep the goals at the front of everybody's mind.

- Track performance and measure output using performance management tools.

- Communicate individual results, provide regular feedback and maintain documentation.

- Empower decision-making and be present to help teams enact their decisions.

- Most importantly, praise success publicly, criticize privately.

14 Hiring

One of the biggest challenges companies face is finding the right talent. The 'war on talent' is a term coined by McKinsey & Company in 1997 which refers to the increasingly competitive challenge of attracting and retaining talent and is still more than ever relevant in the ongoing intensified demographic shifts, twenty years later. Offering people the option to work remotely will give you the edge in attracting the very best people. A survey by Owl Labs reported that fully distributed companies in the US take 33 per cent less time to hire employees compared to traditional ones, and companies that support remote work experience 25 per cent lower employee turnover than those that don't.[1] In this section, we will look at some of the ways you can capitalize on this advantage and build a winning team.

Employer branding

In order to attract top talent, a company must invest in their online employer branding, clearly showcasing the friendly culture and detailing what working there remotely looks like. It's the first interaction a potential candidate has with the hiring company.

People join a company because:

- they love the product and want to be part of the process.

- they love the work environment and the way a company functions.

- they see that the company cares for the wellbeing of its employees.

Candidates will ask current and past employees in their network for advice or recommendations, so:

- Have a profile on LinkedIn, Glassdoor, Twitter, Medium and messaging platforms where relevant. Studies have shown that 83 per cent of job seekers research a company before they apply.[2]

- List members of the team they will work with, not just the leadership, on the website.

Interview process

How does a manager assess a candidate's abilities? The best way is to create a hiring experience that mirrors the way the candidate will be working in order to test whether they will be successful in such an environment. For example, if the position to be filled requires mainly written communication and frequent video calls, then it is important to get an idea of how the candidate would cope using these communication mediums. The interview process for this role would consist of a written part (text-based interview) and a part using video calls, ideally involving team members in them.

It is always highly recommended to have another person

join the interview to provide a second opinion. If this is not possible, recording the interview will enable other team members involved in the selection process to view it in their own time.

Remote jobs are, in theory, open to anyone, anywhere in the world. To avoid an avalanche of applications, job advertisements should include specifications on time zones. The salary range offered for a given position should also be clearly stated.

Behaviour-based interviewing

Behavioural interviewing is a powerful way to understand a person and how they approach their work remotely. This is important when building a remote team because the behaviour of team members and their interactions are even more important when they are in diverse locations.

Ask questions like: 'How do you schedule your day and how do you prioritize tasks?', 'How would you handle lack of face-to-face contact when you work remotely?' or 'If you had an issue when the rest of your remote team was offline, how would you go about solving it?'

According to Toggl, a time-tracking app and remote first company, the main traits that remote companies look for when hiring are self-discipline, great communication skills, strong organization skills and the ability to work effectively in a team environment.[3] Candidates must have the ability to build personal workflow for maximum productivity regardless of the environment, using to-do lists, flow boards and time tracking.

During an interview, Toggl also looks into things that can be learned but are not crucial to making the final decision: the ability to collaborate virtually, attention to transparency and avoiding distraction when working from home. They ask questions about the candidate's personal care skills such as their daily regular break habits and their ability to switch off after work.

A thriving remote worker is:

- a clear communicator

- self-disciplined and comfortable working long periods remotely

- capable of taking the initiative.

Compensation for remote employees

Compensation for remote employees is a very controversial topic. What happens when you have two people doing the same job but living in different cities? Or when an employee moves to a cheaper city than the one they were living in? Creating a fair compensation structure is very important to keep the trust of the team members. Companies will find themselves administratively exhausted if they constantly need to review and update pay structures.

Compensation modelling can use three different approaches: global salary model, local salary model and hybrid salary model.

- Global salary model pays everyone the same compensation irrespective of location.

- Local salary model pays compensation based on a calculation of the local cost of living.

- Hybrid salary model considers different category ranges, taking into account local factors, and is calculated using a multiplier of the most expensive compensation to determine one of three geographic bands: high, average or low cost-of-living area.

Onboarding

Welcoming someone to a remote team

Hiring is only one step of the process when building a remote team. The next part, onboarding, making those hired feel welcome and setting them up for success, is crucial for retaining new employees.

A clear onboarding strategy must be defined, documented and put in place. Each step of the process must be listed, and executed in a manner that ensures the new hire receives all the necessary information to fulfil their role, but is not overwhelmed.

A new office-based employee might be treated to all kinds of social lunches, training programmes and meet-and-greets. You will need to replicate these contacts remotely to familiarize a new remote employee with the company, their role and their team. Mastering remote onboarding is crucial to ensure new team members will thrive.

It is highly advisable to create a company handbook to be accessed by all employees and shared with new hires upon their starting date. The handbook should be a written document setting out the company's goals, values, policies and procedures and any other relevant information to assist employees in doing their work. This document should be drafted as soon as teams go remote, and must be regularly updated as the company grows and policies and procedures evolve. The virtual handbook should include:

- ✓ company's values and mission
- ✓ HR, legal policies and security information
- ✓ code of conduct
- ✓ communication policy
- ✓ organizational chart
- ✓ team directory
- ✓ company benefits
- ✓ holiday and sick leave policies

Each company will have their own onboarding method but below are the three crucial steps to ensure the new hire is properly introduced to the company.

- Step 1: Welcome new hires to the team either by email or through the messaging apps.

- Step 2: Provide the new hire with an appropriate first task/ project. Put some thought into what the new hire will be doing and avoid them having to 'read the docs' or 'join the daily calls'. One of the main reasons why people leave their jobs is because they do not find them challenging enough. By assigning a challenging task to the new hire, you will most likely increase productivity and excitement in their new role. There are two ways to go about this: have the new hire work in a group project which will help them get acquainted with their colleagues; or hand them an individual assignment while they learn the dynamics of the remote team. Usually, a group project would be handled more easily by new hires who already have experience of working with distributed teams. It's your role to ensure that the new hire is adjusting and understands how the team dynamics work.

- Step 3: Check-in with the new hire. Set aside some time after a couple of weeks to follow up on how they are getting on and receive feedback. It is important to capture first impressions as often assumptions are made and rituals or processes may go unquestioned. Best practice would be to carry out two other checks during the new remote team member's first three months as they may have some questions or require extra information on how things are done.

If these check-ins are performed by HR, they should be shared with the new hire's direct superior, but it is highly recommended to involve the team lead in the process.

Fatima's first day as a UX designer

Fatima is very excited to join Cool Block Designs as they have a fantastic reputation, and she was able to move back to her home town from a tiny apartment in Berlin to a nice house and garden.

It is Fatima's first experience in a remote company. To help her prepare, her new manager, Ornelia, had given her access in advance to the company email and shared drives and set her up in the messaging channels.

At 8.30 Fatima has an introduction call with Ornelia, covering which channels are for what, the daily status update by the team at 10.00 every morning and a run-through of what the regular meetings are for. Ornelia gives her a first project to work on, which she is to deliver in two days, and follows up the call with a document outlining the tasks for the next couple of weeks.

At 10.30 there is a group video call with her new colleagues, who introduce themselves and welcome Fatima to the team.

Fatima continues figuring out her first project and makes a start.

At 14.00, Dieter, the HR manager, calls Fatima and takes her through the various policies, how the holiday calendar works and what to do if she is ill, as well as taking down the details of her emergency contacts.

Fatima messages one of her new team members to ask a couple of questions, and they end up having a video call discussing several topics.

The first day feels like a success. With the structured introduction, Fatima already knows her way around a little and has met the team properly. It will help her to learn who does what in the company and where all the useful resources are so she can get up to speed quickly.

At Help Scout, a remote customer care company, they constantly look to invest in social capital by creating virtual opportunities for their team members to get to know each other and make memories. When a new person joins the team, as part of their onboarding, they are asked five questions about themselves, for example, 'What is your favourite music genre?'[4]

These are ways to get conversation started and to help people get to know each other. Help Scout encourage existing employees to reach out to the new hires on their own, too.

To replace the 'watercooler' moment,[5] they use a Slack integration tool called Donut that randomly matches two colleagues once a month and schedules a half-hour virtual coffee date. They also have monthly 'Troop Talks'[6] through Zoom, which are informal gatherings of nine or ten team members structured around a predefined theme. Examples of topics would be favourite new apps, books, movies, series sharing, best recipes. This practice evolved from many failed virtual happy hours, which seemed too forced and unnatural to their team members.

Airtreks, a travel company employing people around the world, use a company orientation checklist to onboard their new hires, making sure every step of the process is completed. Additionally, every new team member is assigned to a job coach and to an orientation leader. During their first weeks, they have daily meetings with their orientation leader and regular check-ins with their job coach to make sure they are equipped with all the information they need to do their work.

Boldly, a subscription staffing company, do things differently. They have created and aggregated all onboarding videos, guides and processes in their intranet and give access to the new hire on day one so they can get acquainted with the company at their own pace. Video meetings are arranged to go through the materials, which include anything from the latest company news to promotional videos and team insights.

Offboarding

In a remote company, each step in an employee's life-cycle holds equal importance, so companies must also design an offboarding strategy. Research by Aberdeen Group, a UK marketing company, found that only 29 per cent of remote organizations have a formal employee exit process, but successful offboarding procedures have a high impact on organizational growth, performance and employee retention and engagement. The main steps in the process are: to understand why people leave, ensure that all projects are properly handed over and revoke digital access.

In a physical office, when someone gives their notice, managers and colleagues still see them every day for the next few weeks. That provides the opportunity to wrap things up, regarding both work and the personal aspect. However, in a remote setting, time can slip away and the exiting employee could leave without a fair closure and a proper handover of transitioning projects.

Exit interviews are the best method to understand why team members are leaving and can be a valuable tool in improving employee retention if feedback and the insights garnered are carefully taken into consideration. It can also allow you to gather information on how the culture of the company is perceived by the employees, which is particularly important in a remote setup, when management can be dissociated from the reality experienced by their teams. Additionally, you give the departed person a chance to express themselves and leave on a positive note with the proper thank you they deserve given the lack of physical proximity in working remotely.

Here is what an offboarding process should look like:

- check-ins until the last day of work to ensure project transition is going smoothly

- exit interview

- recover company assets and revoke digital access

- finalize and sign off relevant documentation.

Part 3 Self-care and Self-organization

15 Daily Practices and Healthy Routines

When working remotely, especially from home, it can be very hard to set the boundaries between personal and professional time. In fact, studies have found that most remote workers struggle with unplugging after work, loneliness and distractions at home.[1] The CEO of Doist, Amir Salihefendic, could not have put it better: 'Remote work isn't just a different way to work – it's a different way to live', and so we need to acknowledge the importance of self-care in a remote setup. Self-care is defined as 'the practice of taking an active role in protecting one's own wellbeing and happiness, in particular during periods of stress'. In this section we show you how to manage and make the most of remote working, with advice on how to care for yourself physically and mentally, and provide tips on how to be on top of your work and enjoy home activities by developing healthy routines.

Personal exercise: take a couple of minutes to do some introspection on the way you work

Below you will find a checklist we have developed for you to make sure you are aware of yourself and your environment and have put in place the right setting and developed the right habits to succeed in your remote work setup.

- What is your place of work?

- Is your workstation equipped with comfortable furniture to work long hours?

- Are you planning breaks from your workstation during the day?

- How do you plan your workdays?

- How do you start your working day?

- How do you end your working day?

- Are you staying active? Eating healthily? Sleeping well?

- Are you taking time off?

- What do you do for yourself?

- What distracts you in your workspace and how do you manage it?

- Are your home and workspace clean?

- Do you sometimes feel lonely, isolated or on the verge of a burnout?

- Are you part of a community outside your work?

- Are you thinking of and planning your career development?

A dedicated workspace

How many hours do you spend in your workspace? Six to eight at least; even longer? Setting up a quality workspace is vital to productivity. It can be a desk in your home, a desk in a co-working space or shared office, or it can be a spot in a local coffee shop – even better, a mix of all of them.

There are lots of misconceptions around what defines an office. According to the Merriam-Webster dictionary, an office is 'the place in which a professional person conducts business'.[2] What constitutes a productive workspace will depend on your workstyle. According to Catherine Avery, owner of productivitybydesign.com, productivity happens only when one sets aside a space for work. She says that if you do not have that dedicated workspace you are not honouring the work you do. It is one of the most common mistakes people make when they are working remotely.[3] Creating your workspace should not be difficult. Choosing a spot in a less used room will work, but avoid having your desk in a place filled with distractions or physically uncomfortable, like a dining table or a bed. Ideally, your workspace should be in a room with a door, so that you can be shut away and interrupted only if needed.

One of the benefits of working remotely is that it gives you the opportunity to change scenery as often as you like. This can be from working three days a week in your designated workspace and two days a week in a coffee shop, or working a couple of days on your patio or dining table and the rest of the time in your designated workspace. Moving from space to space is a strategy for staying focused and productive because it breaks the monotony, which can affect us all occasionally. Brie Reynolds, career development coach and specialist in flexible and remote jobs, promotes these changes of scenery. In an interview in Business Insider, Brie stated that 'different spaces in the home lend themselves to different kinds of work'.[4] No single environment is effective for every task, and alternating environments will boost productivity. It is for this reason that companies are creating hybrid and open spaces that give employees a range of workspaces, which is also the same offering as co-working spaces.

It is very important to set up a dedicated workspace, but also important to have some kind of rotation of work spots to associate different environments with different kinds of work. This will help to keep you fresh, productive and motivated and avoid feeling caught up in an endless loop of workdays that blend into each other monotonously in a strict and inflexible self-imposed routine.

Maintaining good posture

Being able to work wherever you want can also mean settling in places that are not built for work. Some places can be detrimental to the spine. According to the International Labour Office (ILO) 2017 report, one third of remote workers working from home experienced back pain and nearly half experienced neck pain.[5] It is important to ensure that you set up an ergonomic workstation where you can do your work in a comfortable way. Remember that the top line of your screen should be at or just below your eye level, about half a metre from your face to protect your eyes.

It is worth investing in an adjustable ergonomic chair, preferably one on wheels so you can move and change position. Sit–stand desks are becoming more available and affordable. Try out the different models in a furniture shop to make sure you choose the most suitable one for you, depending on your space, workstyles and needs. Look for second-hand markets, as many companies list their furniture when they upgrade or close down. You can also make a request to your employer, as much new legislation around remote work now requires the employer to equip the employee with adequate furniture to deliver the work.

When setting up your home workspace, add some decorations, a plant or a picture. Maybe you'd like to have a whiteboard or a good smart speaker/digital assistant. Make your workstation a nice place to be.

Another source of poor posture can be working in a café. While you have a steady supply of nice drinks (and the odd pastry) and free WiFi, the banquet seating or reclaimed chairs are not designed for prolonged use or work and may lead to discomfort, including a bad back. To avoid this, plan your time in the café to have that nice coffee and pastry while you answer your emails or read the blog posts you have been meaning to catch up on, and then go to the place where you have your comfy, adjustable chair.

Keeping active

The sedentary position is probably the most common occupational disease of our time. Think of a developer or a designer whose task is to be in front of the computer all day. Is that you? It goes without saying that having a co-working space within walking or cycling distance is a good way to get the circulation moving at the start and end of the day. If you're working from home, leave the house, run a small errand, even if you plan to come back soon. This will fend off cabin fever.

In an office setting it is perfectly acceptable to get up to fetch a drink, but in a remote work setting there is a tinge of guilt about being offline for five minutes. Yet the act of getting up and getting a glass of water or something from the fruit bowl, or putting the kettle on, is very beneficial in giving you a break from the screen and, importantly, it brings in light exercise to your day.

Try to take some exercise some time during the day:

- A walk. You could set yourself a goal. 5,000 steps?

- A workout group in a gym or park near you

- A swim if you have a pool nearby

- A bike ride if you have a nice circuit and the sun is shining

- If you are new to running, you could try the couch to 5km programme

- If you already run, you could set yourself a target to improve your 10km time.

You can plan these activities with friends so that you get to socialize throughout your day and see other people outside your home.

Exercising regularly not only keeps you healthy, but also helps you to focus better on your work, reduces stress and increases productivity. One study published in the *International Journal of Workplace Health Management* showed that workday exercise improves general wellbeing, with 72 per cent of participants reporting an improvement in time management and workload completed on days they exercised.[6] Many companies have seen the benefits to their employees' productivity of exercising during the workday: giants like Google and Lone have in-office gyms with yoga classes in the workplace.[7]

Remote companies are adapting to this change by offering access to online workout classes or gym memberships. At Global Upside, an HR solutions company in the US, live sessions and recordings of yoga and high intensity interval training (HIIT) classes are available to employees three times a week.

Organize and plan your day

Setting your personal objectives into Work, Self and Home categories (weekly, monthly and quarterly) will help you stay motivated and achieve what needs to be done. Practice time-blocking on your calendar to prioritize your tasks and allocate time for things that are important, whether for work or for yourself. This self-management productivity method is very effective as it promotes the state of deep work and not only makes you aware of how you spend your time but also helps you estimate the time needed for future work. The two most frequently used ways of practising time-blocking are task-batching or day-theming.

Task-batching, grouping similar tasks together during a dedicated time period, helps you manage and get through urgent daily tasks.

For example, every weekday morning:

- 9.00 to 10.00: answering emails

- 10.00 to 11.00: call with the teams with the daily status

- 11.00 to 12.30: research

Day-theming is assigning an allocated day to work on specific tasks that are grouped in themes. For example:

- Monday: administrative tasks
- Tuesday: client and project work
- Wednesday: training day
- Thursday: client and project work
- Friday: research.

| Figure 3: Task-batching[8]

TASK-BATCHING SCHEDULE

	Light Concentration	Moderate Concentration	Deep Concentration	BREAK

8 a.m.	Email
8.30 a.m.	**Client Sales Calls**
9.30 a.m.	Writing for Blog
10.30 a.m.	Research
12 p.m.	**LUNCH BREAK**
1 p.m.	**Meeting**
2 p.m.	**Meeting**
2.30 p.m.	**BREAK**
2.45 p.m.	Editing
4 p.m.	Email
4.30 p.m.	**Preparation**

This can also be applied to household chores. For example, some people like to do the cooking for a whole week, freeze the meals and then reheat them as required. From a remote perspective, the best way to be as productive as possible is to align your work and home tasks in a planner, whether it be by task-batching or day-theming. Try each method and see which one works best for you, or juggle both. You must be flexible and realize that sometimes schedules have to be changed or external help might be required.

| Figure 4: Day-theming[9]

Sunday	Monday	Tuesday	Wednesday	Thursday	Friday	Saturday
Planning Day	Admin Day	Writing Day	Audio/Video Day	Training Day	Deep Work Day	Family Day

Tim Ferris, one of the most popular authors on the subject of productivity, shares many recommendations in his bestseller *The 4-Hour Workweek* on how to escape the nine-to-five workdays and live anywhere. He maintains that there is a big difference between being productive and being busy. He advocates focusing on measuring one's results in terms of time spent and finding ways to eliminate less important time-consuming tasks. He recommends applying the 80/20 rule in all daily tasks. Also known as the 'Pareto Principle', it states that 80 per cent of results come from 20 per cent of time and effort. Identify the tasks that you should drop and focus on what makes you productive and successful.[10]

Make sure you not only organize your days in advance but also know when you are at your most productive and prioritize the tasks that have a higher rate of success.

The end-of-day ritual

Some people may work from a co-working space and others fully from home, but in both cases there has to be a clear end to the day, an end-of-day ritual, because how you end your day is as important as how you start it. When working in an office, the commute forms a natural break between home and the workplace; when working remotely it is good to continue with the same rhythm, although there are far more pleasant ways to do this than being squashed in a train or crawling in traffic.

Practising this ritual will help you better manage and enjoy your work–life balance. You will feel less stressed at the end of your day, motivated to start off the next one knowing what tasks are unfinished and where to concentrate energy and time to complete them. Each person develops their own personal ritual but the main points should be to review the to-do list of the day and amend if needed the plan for the next day. Knowing your priorities in advance and what the following day will look like will reduce any stress. Then tidy up your desk so that you can start off fresh tomorrow.

The evolution of technology has made it easier for all employees, remote and not, to take their work everywhere, check their emails, reply to messages and make themselves available to take a call, even on holiday. When you are remote, this can happen frequently and can become a bad habit because you do not follow the natural cycle that is set in physical offices where people go to and leave their desks around the same time. Learning to unplug from work can have a real impact on work–life balance. Getting it wrong and finding it difficult to call it a day after work is a great concern in remote working as it can lead to burnout. Turn off your notifications and stop checking your emails after a certain time. Practise an end-of-day ritual.

To combat the 'always on' culture of checking company messages and emails some companies enforce a ban on out-of-hours emails. Volkswagen did so in 2012.[11] Governments are also implementing 'right to disconnect' policies. In 2017, France introduced a law giving employees of companies with over fifty staff the right to negotiate out-of-hours work activity, including the right not to have access to emails at specified times.[12] In 2019, authorities in New York discussed proposals to become the first city in the US to grant employees the 'right to disconnect' after work.[13] Though disconnecting from work is very important, some argue that the enforced banning of email by companies is too blunt and that people feel more empowered when they are in control of their workload. For instance, they might decide to take an hour to enjoy a run, then work later in the evening to make up the time missed, and that work may rely on email.

WELLBEING TIPS

- Schedule regular breaks by setting alarms or using a wearable, such as a Fitbit, for example. Call someone on the phone.

- Schedule some time to work out. Now that you don't spend time commuting, use this time to do some exercise.

- Keep a consistent work and sleep schedule.

- Get out of your home. You need to have a social life. Co-working spaces can help but you can also attend different events in your area to socialize with other people.

- Learn to cook at home.

- Instead of checking Facebook/Twitter/Instagram during your downtime, use the time to clean. Do this often enough and it'll make your weekends freer and less stressful.

- Make sure you take your holidays, and where possible switch off from all technology. It can be scary but it is rewarding not to check a device regularly, even if it is just for a long weekend.

16 Wellbeing in Practice

We researched how companies are putting wellbeing into practice. Global Upside, an HR solutions company headquartered in San José, California, with over 500 employees across the world, 50 per cent of them in remote locations, have made sure that all their staff (and their families) can access an employee assistance programme with a focus on work–life balance. This programme, which is strictly confidential and personalized, is delivered through a web application and it includes unlimited access to counsellors and specialists in the areas of family welfare, health and wellness, emotional wellbeing, daily living and work–life balance. It gives employees access to a wide range of legal and financial assistance through specialized consultants. Global strongly believe that they should provide their employees with support when it comes to their personal life. On a regular basis they send out baskets of goodies to their employees' homes in recognition of their work for the company. This kind of reward is commonplace for companies and is usually very well received by employees, especially those in a remote setup, as they are made to feel they are not alone, not forgotten, but are appreciated and taken care of.

Many companies with remote employees are investing in the mental wellbeing of their staff. An online therapy platform company based in Madrid, ifeelonline.com, is often the option of choice. Emotional support for companies' employees is available through automated tools, chat messaging or video calls. 'Companies nowadays are rightfully placing more importance on the emotional wellbeing of their teams as a way of promoting individual growth outside the professional context. It's a fundamental aspect of company strategy, and plays a significant role in talent attraction and retention,' said Martin Villanueva Ordás, co-founder and COO of ifeel, in a 2020 interview with the authors.

17   Eating and Sleeping

Eating healthily

It is worth emphasizing that working remotely requires a lot of discipline. Not having a structure or an established daily routine will not only affect your productivity but also the choices you make around your diet. On a good day, working remotely means being productive and going through eight hours of uninterrupted work, exercising in the morning and eating a healthy lunch. On a bad day, you can be in pyjamas all day, raiding the fridge and struggling to focus on your work. Diet is an important factor in being productive and can't be factored out. The WHO reports that 'adequate nourishment can raise national productivity levels by 20 per cent on average.'[1] You will be better able to focus and accomplish tasks when you have eaten properly.

We have discussed the benefits of task-batching in planning your days. The same principle applies to planning your meals. Batch-cooking meals over the weekend or any week night is a great way to save time by cutting down on daily kitchen time and also helps you eat better. Having prepared meals ready in the fridge or freezer at home removes the temptation to pick up or order fast food. According to *BBC Good Food*, this also leads to big savings.[2] What is not to like about that?

A good night's sleep

Working remotely with people in different time zones can affect your sleep schedule because you may have to stay up late to connect with your colleagues and any unresolved matters may dwell on your mind through the night.

Set yourself a schedule and stick to it. Only you know when you're most productive, so decide according to whatever works best with your productivity. Have a work and a home phone and laptop, so you can switch off your work phone and laptop as you would when you leave the office. Your colleagues and customers do not expect a reply out of hours, but often will include you in discussions with the intention that you will catch up when you are online next. Never check your work phone last thing at night or when you wake up. Start your day with some exercise, a shower and a bite to eat before you switch on.

18 Taking Time Off

Remote workers tend to take less time off than people who are in the office. Although 67 per cent of remote companies have over four weeks of annual holiday allowance, according to Buffer 2019 State of Remote Work report, remote workers take only two to three weeks of holidays per year.[1] This may be a little under reported as some people are likely to take advantage of the flexibility that remote work offers, which allows work while travelling, also known as 'workation'. A workation can combine some time working with fitting in a swim at lunchtime and a nice walk on the beach after work, or a couple of runs down the mountain in the morning before switching on the laptop. While this can be pleasant, it is no substitute for switching off for a week.

It is strongly recommended that you make the most of whatever the company's holiday policy is and use your full allowance. It is very important to take days off, recharge and spend time with family and friends so that you are more productive upon your return.

19 Nurturing Your Development

According to the 2020 GitLab report,[1] 24 per cent of over 3,000 people interviewed believed they were at a disadvantage in working at home and not being physically with the rest of the team because they saw their career development being hindered, with fewer opportunities of progression. If you are a member of a partially remote team or working remotely with a team that is onsite, it is quite common to feel forgotten.

To make yourself more visible, you don't need to learn new skills or how to market yourself, rather it is a matter of following a couple of practical steps to ensure you are not forgotten or excluded from the discussions.

- Take time to prepare for your meetings with your manager in order to include everything you have accomplished, what challenges you have faced and where you need extra support.

- Take active part in discussions and meetings. If the technology fails in a meeting room, for example if the microphones are bad or not working, it is perfectly all right to ask that the technology issue be fixed or the meeting room changed.

If, as a remote worker or someone who works from home regularly in a hybrid model, you are being ignored, or not included, you may want to look elsewhere for a role in a company that does remote working well. But before you think about that, raise your concerns. It is very likely that those onsite are unaware of the situation as it does not impact them in the same way. In a fully remote team you may find that your colleagues may have the same issues.

For remote workers in co-working centres there are great networking opportunities. Onlinemarketing.de point out that in a co-working centre you might not only meet people from the same industry, which can bring you professional benefits, but also people in different industries whose services you might require one day.[2]

Co-working centres host social events and talks by expert speakers. For example, Full Node[3] in Berlin state their mission is 'to increase the educational, social, and collaborative value to our local community through workshops, events, and meetups'.

There are also good networking opportunities in virtual conferences, which have multiple 'stages' with speaker panels and networking rooms where you can drop in and introduce yourself. The advantage of a virtual conference is that there are no geographical restrictions so it is far less onerous to attend as you do not have to travel or stay in a hotel.

20 Cultivating a Community

As a remote worker, you have the opportunity to build a community of like-minded people with other remote workers. There are plenty of ways to create or be part of a community, through membership in a nearby co-working space or online. The most common are:

- Take a membership in a nearby co-working space.

- Engage on social media with niche groups and professional circles (skill- or location-based) that can be found on Facebook and LinkedIn, for example.

- Attend in person events in your area such as meetups or local conferences that might be of interest.

- Explore special-interest groups centred on one of your hobbies, a sport or field of study.

Remote working does not mean you have to be solo all the time. Not only will joining a community make you feel more involved and connected, it will also expand your social life and that can feed back positively into your professional life through networking, and nurture your career development.

Tomasso – an old hand at remote working

Tomasso has a desk at home set up just as he likes it and he has bought a comfy chair that he can adjust. He has learned how to set up his chair quickly at the co-working centre near his house.

Tomasso likes to go to the co-working centre every day and usually cycles there as it provides secure bike storage. In the summer he takes a longer route home that snakes through the woods by a river.

A Tai Chi group at the co-working centre meets on Tuesdays and Thursdays for a session at the local park. It is good to get out for exercise at lunchtime and it has a convivial social element.

Tomasso has some contact with customers in San Francisco, which is a challenge for someone based in a different time zone, but thankfully they are understanding and do not expect him to be around at odd times for calls. They record their calls for Tomasso to watch later.

Tomasso has got to know a few people at the co-working centre, not just the Tai Chi club members but some he met at the social events and afterwork meetups that have been organized around topics related to his design work.

He balances his work with exercise and social interaction, and makes sure he sets boundaries around his day.

21 Your Working Environment

Blurring the boundaries of home

Home is the safe space where you are with the people you care about, it is the place you return to after a day in the office and change into comfortable clothes, it is where you can be yourself. We all have a personal self and a professional self; the personal is the social self who likes the people around them and needs to be liked, whereas the professional self is more concerned about being good at what we do and wanting respect and recognition. These are clearly not binary and there is a degree of overlap, for instance being sociable and friendly at work, although there may be less overlap with the professional self at home. The dynamics shift in the context of remote working, when you have to be your professional self at home, usually the setting for the personal self.

It is important in a personal relationship to recognize that it is the personal self that is involved in the relationship, not the professional self. When both you and your partner are your professional selves at home, you have to find ways to disconnect and revert to your personal selves. How can you switch? Can you both do it at the same time or do the boundaries blur? It puts a strain on any relationship if you and your partner share a dining room or kitchen table as your remote office. The complexities of your professional and personal selves are intertwined, and while you love your partner's personal self, their professional self may be more difficult to understand. The only exception to this might be a couple who met at work and know both the personal and professional sides of each other and are happy enough to work together.

If space permits, it is nice to set up a dedicated area for work that each person can call 'the office'. Depending on your creativity, it could be stylish office 'sheds' for the garden or making a space out of a garage, or simply adapting corners of rooms in the house. This then gives the couple the freedom to be their professional selves and, when they meet in the kitchen for lunch, to switch to their personal selves and have the different space in which to be social, loving and enjoy each other's company. This may not work for everyone, and perhaps more flexibility may be required. For instance, you could swap the workspaces you create in the home from time to time to have a change or to make it fair if one space is more cramped or in a colder room.

22 Managing Distractions

A positive aspect of working remotely is that you avoid work-place distractions such as meetings and colleagues' interruptions, but working from home comes with its own distractions. You have to be prepared and learn how to manage home distractions, such as children, flatmates, pets and housework. The good thing is that in most cases it is easier to create boundaries at home to control distractions than it is to avoid interruptions in the office.

Housework

Keep your house or flat clean and tidy to create a nice environment to work in.

One of the perks of working at home is that you can fit some housework into your work schedule, for instance loading or emptying the dishwasher, hanging up clothes from a wash, or preparing lunch. It is OK to do it, but don't let it take over your day.

Doing some small chores during the day gets you out of your chair and gives you a break. You could still be thinking about a work problem and creativity might strike!

An inventive way to use your washing machine, dishwasher

or any other household electronic machine is as your work timer. Commit yourself to completing one task or project during a wash cycle, and this can train you to get into a deep work state and be more productive.

With some organization and practice, fitting housework into your workday will become easier and you will quickly find out what works best for you. If not, then you might consider hiring some help. Think 'Clean house = clean mind'!

Children and flatmates

Most of us who work at home will have someone else in the house when we are working, even if it is only for part of the day or week. Establish ground rules for flatmates, partners or adult relatives and ask them to communicate with you using messaging apps as if you were not at home, so you can respond in your breaks. Set boundaries on when they can interrupt you and when they cannot. Sharing your agenda of calls with the family will help avoid interruptions, but you must also stay flexible and acknowledge that you may be interrupted on occasions. Be polite and explain you want to finish something, but accept that it may not always be possible.

If you are a recent parent, do not try to work and do full-time childcare; you will not do either very well. It is tempting as a remote worker to imagine that, because you have your workplace set up at home, you can carry on as before now you have a baby. Sure, everyone is thrilled for you and the new arrival, and you can beam with pride during one of your regular video calls. But can you cope when the little one howls in the background and you have to cut short the meeting to deal with them?

Older children should be taught the difference between wanting and needing your attention. You could try using a sign on your door indicating when they can interrupt and when you must not be disturbed. Build in short breaks with the kids before they force themselves on you. If that becomes an impediment to your work, maybe consider hiring help during your busiest working hours.

23 Work–Life Balance

It should be obvious what work–life balance means: how you juggle personal time for relationships, family responsibilities and outside interests and hobbies and time for work. But many professionals struggle to get it right.

It is important that you do not let work take over, and you must be disciplined in setting boundaries around your working day. As we have discussed, creating routines such as a daily walk or cycle ride before work helps to do so if you are home-based. As does observing end-of-day rituals, and ensuring you have a separate phone and laptop for work and home so that if you check the news on your phone while eating breakfast you don't then start reading the Slack or Teams messages or get interrupted by emails. The Doist blog[1] suggests customizing your notifications so you deal only with emails that set off specific ringtones.

We have discussed how to manage distractions and not let them get in the way of a productive day, as well as the need to build in breaks to your day, have a healthy lunch and eat fruit not biscuits (well, the odd biscuit doesn't harm!).

What is important is to remember that the work–life balance is exactly that. While you have home things you would like to do during working hours, you should consider the business needs first. Conversely, occasionally you may have to make alternative personal arrangements to accommodate work. It is not good practice to take thirty minutes here and there for various errands or chores and yet not make up the time. The balance in this case has not reached a fair equilibrium. On the other hand, if you have been working longer to meet an important deadline, then it is acceptable to ask to finish a little earlier once the deadline is passed, and thus keep the balance.

Balancing work and life is achievable but beware that one does not dominate the other. If work is tipping too far, talk to your colleagues and bring it up in your weekly meeting with your manager. If you are under pressure at home, let your manager know that you have some personal things to deal with. If the pressure is constant, you must seek to reduce it. For example, you might find an after-school club for your children a couple of evenings a week to give you some precious time to get your work done, or perhaps start an hour earlier so you can afford the time to, say, take the kids to football.

24 Mental Care

Your mental health

Working from home, you can easily feel disconnected since you don't have the same opportunities to interact with other people that you would in an office. The good news is that this is preventable.

It is important that you identify whether you are feeling isolated or lonely or both. Loneliness is about missing people and social interactions; a typical sufferer would be someone living alone, who works from home and has food or groceries delivered. Isolation is the feeling that you are cut off, and can manifest itself in remote teams, for instance when communication is not working as well as it should and some of the team are being excluded or isolated.

Burnout, a systemic problem caused by overworking, can also adversely affect your mental health.

We cannot stress enough how important it is to be in touch with yourself, overcome feelings of loneliness, avoid isolation and recognize the initial signs of burnout. Most important for achieving a successful work–life balance is to put your mental health first.

Dealing with loneliness

Loneliness can be a problem when working remotely, as it arises from the lack of interaction with others, limited social contact and just sitting alone in the same place for a prolonged time. According to Buffer 2020 State of Remote Work report, 20 per cent of those working remotely struggle with loneliness.[1] Loneliness and difficulty with communication and collaboration are the two most common challenges workers face in a remote setting.

There are several ways to mitigate this. First, work in a co-working space where you are surrounded by others in a similar situation. Make the effort to get to know the people around you by attending co-working events, or simply start a conversation with the person in the seat next to you. You might be surprised at how like-minded your co-workers are and that you have shared interests. You could discover through them more things to do in the neighbourhood or acquire new contacts and clients related with your job.

Another way to combat loneliness is to ensure you hear real voices by talking to family and friends daily by phone or video. Not only does it help to prevent the feeling of loneliness, but it also keeps you updated and involved in what is happening. It is very important as well to talk to other team members and peers when you start feeling lonely. Speaking up will help you to understand why you are feeling this way and what would make you feel better. Often breaking out of the structured daily routine and amending it to suit you better will help.

Coping with isolation

Isolation is complicated and can be more difficult to deal with than loneliness. Communication shortcomings can lead to team members being excluded. It may simply be the case that a subset of the team are working on a knotty problem for which they have the necessary expertise.

There are a few simple ways to mitigate isolation. Speak to your boss and explain that you are busy with the work but have no interaction with the rest of the team. There should be regular meetings where everyone is included. Maybe the boss cancelled them, thinking that as everyone is involved in working through an issue a meeting is not necessary; you can point out that it is not the case.

With hybrid teams where some are office based, or a sub-group who all work in the same co-working centre, care must be taken to include the remote team members. Measures could be as simple as having a short informal get-together for a chat on a video call, or it might be that a structured timetable is required, setting out a time for remote workers to meet with the office-based or co-working team at a regular interval.

Being outside the office can also bring the feeling of isolation when the infrastructure is missing: for instance, there is no handy IT person to come and sort out your laptop, or you cannot drop by accounts with a fistful of receipts and your monthly expenses form. A company can remedy this by having a 'remote-first' policy, so that everyone files expenses online and uploads their receipts, or you have the friendly IT person in the co-working space or, even better, the IT team are able to remote analyse your laptop or send you a replacement if the hard drive blows up.

A subtle form of isolation is the feeling of being overlooked by your manager when it comes to recognition for your successes, or perhaps promotion is taking longer than for your peers. To be recognized for project successes may need a bit of communication input by you, not to brag about what a marvellous job you are doing but just to give others a short update on what you have achieved. Promotion is discussed in the career progression section (p. 87).

Avoiding burnout

Burnout, according to Christina Maslach, a social psychologist at the University of California, Berkeley, results from a systemic combination of overwhelming work exhaustion, detachment from the job and feelings of cynicism that drives a sense of ineffectiveness and lack of accomplishment[2] that translates into a stressful experience.

Remote workers are particularly at risk of burnout because of their isolation and lack of face-to-face communication. They are more prone to work exhaustion as well because they are constantly looking to prove their worth, which can trigger an inability to unplug from work.

Signs and symptoms of burnout:[3]

- Feeling alienated from work-related activities, which may cause stress or frustrations with your job. This might result in feeling cynical about the job and distancing yourself emotionally from your organization.

- Physical symptoms of chronic stress include severe headaches, stomach ache and intestinal issues.

- Emotional symptoms of exhaustion are feeling constantly tired and drained, and lacking energy to cope and get the work done.

It is very important to be aware of these signs, as not only do they affect your work but they can also spill into other areas of family life and social relationships and impact negatively on your wellbeing. Take care not to let yourself reach that point.

Whenever you feel stressed and exhausted, take a couple of days off and ask yourself whether you are lonely, disconnected or overworked. Talk about it, first with your close circle and then with your manager. Inform yourself about any employee programme that can assist you during this time or seek professional help.

To prevent burnout, make sure you are taking care of yourself:

- Exercise, take regular short breaks, sleep well and eat healthily.

- Organize your day.

- Unplug from work by practising an end-of-day ritual.

- Take time off.

- Make sure you have a good work–life balance.

25 Video Call Fatigue

In a blog from the World Economic Forum, researchers and experts in the field of communications stated that video conferencing can lead to stress and exhaustion.[1] There are several reasons why video calls are tiring: they increase self-awareness and the desire to project a good image; they require greater concentration than face-to-face conversations in order to pick up people's non-verbal cues; and staring at a screen for a long time is fatiguing, with multi-person screens exacerbating the problem. In an article in *Scientific American*, it was observed that call participants concentrate much more on the person talking than in a face-to-face conversation, for fear that looking somewhere else may give the impression of lack of interest. Prolonged eye contact through the screen will cause the brain to overreact.[2]

To avoid video call fatigue, schedule your video calls appropriately and try to build in breaks between calls. Avoid having a full day of video calls where possible. Turn on video only for essential meetings, as not all calls need video and it is important to decide when to switch to a phone call or email. You don't always have to put your camera on; don't feel pressured to do so.

As a guide, with six or fewer participants video can be helpful as these calls tend to be more focused meetings requiring a higher degree of interaction. For calls with more than six people, it is good practice not to have the video camera switched on and to be on mute as these are often knowledge-sharing calls with short updates from selected participants.

Video conferencing does not need to last an hour. Video calls are usually set up for an hour because that was how long office meetings used to last, as people had to travel to attend the meeting and it is courteous to the attendees to factor in that time. Today, there is no reason why a video call cannot be just fifteen minutes long.

If your call is not a video conference and does not require the camera to be on or material at hand, consider doing 'walking meetings'. This simply means what it says: you walk about while you hold your meeting. Recent research, published in the *Harvard Business Review*, concluded that walking leads to an increase in creative thinking and keeps you active.[3]

The bookcase as a statement?

Video calls have given rise to a fascination with people's bookcases. For some it is a great way to project an image of seriousness; others fear in horror that people will find yet another way to judge them. The Twitter account Bookcase Credibility,[4] with over 100,000 followers and the tagline *What you say is not as important as the bookcase behind you*, illustrates the trend for people's interest in celebrities, politicians, academics and TV pundits and what their bookcases say about them.

It is very hard to read the titles of the books in a normal video call, although some book covers are very distinctive and it can be a sport for people to figure out what books are on the shelves. Perhaps you can entertain yourself with it on long calls.

There are countless style and design guides on the internet on how to arrange your books, by height or colour, and even specifying the spacing of the books. Do you leave the shelves as they are? Order some antique volumes? Make sure you have a visible display of highbrow books? Can the kids' books stay? It may be less important than you think.

You have a choice: you can project the image you want with a bookshelf or use the option in Zoom or Teams to set a background to hide your bookshelf and make an altogether different statement. Perhaps the best statement is the *Work Remotely* book in a prominent position to show you have mastered remote working?

Conclusion – The Future of Remote Working

Are we ready to go remote? Clearly some people who have experienced remote working on the kitchen table or in a tiny guest room hastily converted to a home office may be less convinced. Those who have tried a badly designed co-working space or attempted to work in a noisy café will also be sceptical.

Small adjustments, the right equipment and adapting to video calls will ensure demand for remote working will increase. There will also be a better understanding from management that people can be trusted as work continues to be delivered by a team that is remotely located.

What will drive the adoption of remote working? The impetus will come from people choosing to work remotely, as companies will follow the talent. Businesses will examine why they are in an expensive city and question whether they need to have everyone in a central office. Businesses that adapt and embrace remote working will have an advantage.

While remote working allows the individual to choose, first, where they live and then where they work, a crucial factor will be the availability of co-working centres. There are two main challenges to the wide-scale adoption of co-working centres for remote workers: first, the open plan design is not the best configuration as evidenced in co-working and centralized workplaces; second, who pays for the co-working centre? The remote worker has the option to work at home for no additional cost and the lack of social contact is seen as a small price to pay. However, if the company were to offer a co-working centre allowance as part of the employment package, then the dynamics will change. Co-working centres will become more widespread throughout smaller cities, towns and even villages.

What might future technology allow us to do? Interestingly, VR and AR technology has been around for a while but has not been adopted for immersive video calling, but perhaps cameras and streaming will evolve so people would appear. The big question is whether it really solves a problem or whether incremental improvements to video conferencing and integrated messaging will dominate.

There is a parallel movement to remote working, and it is happening in the blockchain world. Out of the spotlight of the frantic trading of Bitcoin and the flash-in-the-pan ICOs in 2017, there are groups now working on decentralized autonomous organizations (DAO). This is harnessed to technology which is decentralized by definition and, using the capability of smart contracts, introduces governance through rule-based constitutions. These organizations are still in their infancy, but they are evolving rapidly through the development of tools to model complex systems; these experiments give rise to some interesting ideas and innovations. Why does this relate to remote working? In some ways organizations seeking to structure themselves as totally remote are effectively decentralized, and this is where the parallels begin. As the DAOs evolve and credible decentralized organizations emerge, this could lead to remotely organized companies revisiting how they are structured and how they work.

The future is bright, and remote working will be the main way we work.

Resources

Articles, blogs, websites

https://medium.com/point-nine-news/exit-interviews-a58771573d6e
https://content.remote.tools/
https://www.lionstep.com/sense-belonging-among-remote-employees/
https://www.fastcompany.com/90423310/how-proximity-bias-holds-employees-and-workplaces-back
https://www.coworkingresources.org/

Remote job boards

https://remotewoman.com
https://weworkremotely.com/
https://nodesk.co/remote-jobs/europe/
https://remoteok.io (technical roles mainly)
https://skillcrush.com/blog/sites-finding-remote-work/
https://flexjobs.com
https://www.workingnomads.co/jobs
https://justremote.co/
https://europeremotejobs.com/
https://remoteyear.com/

List to compare cities

https://nomadlist.com/

Impact of the commute to a central office calculator
http://tools.govloop.com/telework-calculator.php
https://mobilitylabel.com/en/#office-location

Co-living/Co-working
http://restation.co/

Notes

Introduction

1 https://www.flexjobs.com/blog/post/flexjobs-2018-annual-survey-workers-believe-flexible-remote-job-can-help-save-money-reduce-stress-more/

2 https://productiveleaders.com/telecommuting-business-profits/

3 https://www.ilo.org/wcmsp5/groups/public/---dgreports/---dcomm/---publ/documents/publication/wcms 544138.pdf

4 https://www.marketwatch.com/story/heres-how-much-your-company-pays-to-rent-office-space-2015-05-27

5 https://www.wsj.com/articles/when-its-time-to-go-back-to-the-office-will-it-still-be-there-11589601618

6 https://globalworkplaceanalytics.com/telecommuting-statistics

7 https://www.flexjobs.com/blog/post/big-numbers-the-environmental-savings-from-telecommuting/

8 https://www.fastcompany.com/90285582/everyone-hates-open-plan-offices-heres-why-they-still-exist; https://www.forbes.com/sites/jiawertz/2019/06/30/open-plan-work-spaces-lower-productivity-employee-morale/#56bfa49261cd; https://royalsocietypublishing.org/doi/full/10.1098/rstb.2017.0239

1 How We Work

1 http://assets.regus.com/pdfs/iwg-workplace-survey/iwg-workplace-survey-2019.pdf

2 https://www.theguardian.com/cities/galley/2016/jun/08/how-far-distance-workers-commute-uk-cities-mapped

3 https://www.case1euro.it/

4 https://www.gigeconomydata.org/basics/what-gig-worker

5 https://blog.hubspot.com/marketing/inspiring-company-mission-statements

6 Sony strapline at https://www.linkedin.com/company/sony/

7 https://www.clifbar.com/who-we-are/

8 https://www.helpscout.com/blog/remote-team-meetings/

9 https://www.ft.com/content/bc8f9c5c-12a3-11ea-a225-db2f231cfeae

10 https://www.glassdoor.com/employers/blog/diversity/

11 https://www.gov.uk/workplace-bullying-and-harassment

12 https://about.gitlab.com/company/team/org-chart/

13 https://www.mailerlite.com/about

14 http://knowledge.wharton.upenn.edu/article/is-your-team-too-big-too-small-whats-the-right-number-2/

15 https://www.sciencedirect.com/science/article/abs/pii/002210317490033X

16 https://www.simplypsychology.org/social-loafing.html

17 https://www.theguardian.com/technology/2018/apr/24/the-two-pizza-rule-and-the-secret-of-amazons-success

18 https://sloanreview.mit.edu/article/what-is-a-chief-knowledge-officer/

2 How We Communicate

1 https://twist.com/remote-work-guides/remote-team-communication#use-cases-for-synchronous-communication

2 https://hbr.org/2016/01/collaborative-overload

3 https://www.standard.co.uk/tech/slack-london-data-lockdown-connect-a4479976.html

4 https://hbr.org/2016/01/collaborative-overload

5 https://www.calnewport.com/books/deep-work/

6 https://toggl.com/blog/flow-state-work

7 Csikszentmihalyi, Mihaly (1996), *Creativity: Flow and the Psychology of Discovery and Invention*, New York, NY: Harper Perennial

8 https://doist.com/blog/asynchronous-communication/

9 https://doist.com/blog/asynchronous-communication/

3 How We Meet

1 https://www.mentimeter.com/

2 https://kahoot.com/business/

3 https://remotehub.io/remote-companies-with-company-retreats

4 http://cryptoplaza.es/

5 https://www.fullnode.berlin/

6 https://www.chainwork.com/

7 https://podcasts.apple.com/es/podcast/hidden-brain/id1028908750?l=en&i=1000498899250

8 SIM hacking can be used to intercept the secure codes: https://www.pandasecurity.com/mediacenter/security/sim-hijacking-explained

9 https://www.wsj.com/articles/fraudsters-use-ai-to-mimic-ceos-voice-in-unusual-cybercrime-case-11567157402

10 https://www.jabra.co.uk/business/speakerphones/jabra-speak-series

11 https://www.logitech.com/en-gb/room-solutions

5 Collaboration and Communication

1 https://www.gallup.com/workplace/268076/manage-loneliness-isolation-remote-workers.aspx

2 https://basecamp.com/guides/how-we-communicate

3 https://www.digitaltrends.com/cool-tech/use-more-emojis-working-from-home/

4 https://frontapp.com/blog/using-emojis-professionally-at-work

6 Hybrid Teams

1 https://blog.trello.com/hybrid-work-guide

8 Outcomes-driven Management

1 https://weekdone.com/
2 https://www.hubspot.com/

9 Goal Setting and Accountability

1 https://blog.rechargepayments.com/how-to-thrive-as-a-fully-remote-company/
2 https://research.tilburguniversity.edu/en/publications/moving-from-individual-to-constructive-accountability

10 Measuring Performance

1 https://felipecastro.com/en/okr/what-is-okr/
2 https://blog.doist.com/how-doist-works-remote/
3 https://engineering.atspotify.com/2014/03/27/spotify-engineering-culture-part-1/
4 https://medium.com/@ericandrews603/spotify-doesnt-use-okrs-anymore-should-you-3927eeaa22dd
5 Taleb, Nassim Nicholas (2013), *Antifragile*, London, Penguin Books
6 https://www.groovehq.com/blog/one-on-one-meetings-for-company-culture
7 https://blog.hubstaff.com/measuring-employee-satisfaction-with-survey/

11 Decision-making

1 http://opensource.guide/starting-a-project/
2 https://opensource.com/article/17/12/asynchronous-decision-making

12 Conflict Resolution

1 https://www.nytimes.com/2006/09/24/books/chapters/0924-1st-peas.html

14 Hiring

1 https://www.owllabs.com/state-of-remote-work

2 https://www.glassdoor.com/employers/blog/6-hr-recruiting-stats-you-need-to-know-for-2018-and-beyond/

3 https://toggl.com/track/out-of-office-building-a-team/

4 https://toggl.com/track/out-of-office-growing-remote-teams/

5 https://recruitingsocial.com/2017/12/help-scout-remote-culture/

6 https://www.helpscout.com/blog/virtual-team-building/

15 Daily Practices and Healthy Routines

1 https://buffer.com/state-of-remote-work-2019

2 https://www.merriam-webster.com/dictionary/office

3 https://www.kentucky.com/news/business/article211602939.html

4 https://www.businessinsider.com/productivity-hack-working-from-home-2017-6

5 https://www.ilo.org/wcmsp5/groups/public/---dgreports/---dcomm/---publ/documents/publication/wcms_544138.pdf

6 https://www.emerald.com/insight/content/doi/10.1108/17538350810926534/full/html

7 https://smallbusiness.chron.com/yoga-classes-workplace-1346.html

8 https://mint.intuit.com/blog/relationships/task-batching-5996/

9 https://doist.com/blog/time-blocking/

10 Ferriss, Timothy (2007), *The 4-hour Work Week: Escape 9–5, Live Anywhere, and Join the New Rich*, New York, NY: Crown Publishers

11 https://www.bbc.co.uk/news/technology-16314901

12 https://www.personneltoday.com/hr/uk-follow-french-introduce-right-disconnect/

13 https://www.laboremploymentlawblog.com/2018/03/articles/
    employer-scheduling-practices/unplug-electronic-
    communications/

17 Eating and Sleeping
1   https://mindflash.com/blog/does-the-food-we-eat-affect-our-
    productivity
2   https://www.bbcgoodfood.com/howto/guide/healthy-batch-
    cooking-recipes

18 Taking Time Off
1   https://buffer.com/state-of-remote-work-2019

19 Nurturing Your Development
1   https://page.gitlab.com/rs/194-VVC-221/images/the-remote-work-
    report-by-gitlab.pdf
2   https://onlinemarketing.de/karriere/new-work/coworking-
    spaces-arbeitsplatz-flexibilitaet-inspiration-networking
3   https://www.fullnode.berlin/events/

23 Work–Life Balance
1   https://blog.doist.com/5-powerful-techniques-achieve-work-life-
    balance/

24 Mental Care
1   https://buffer.com/state-of-remote-work-2020
2   https://www.ncbi.nlm.nih.gov/pmc/articles/PMC4911781/
3   https://www.webmd.com/balance/ss/slideshow-signs-burnout

25 Video Call Fatigue
1   https://www.weforum.org/agenda/2020/05/zoom-fatigue-video-
    conferencing-coronavirus/

2 https://www.scientificamerican.com/article/eye-contact-how-long-
  is-too-long/
3 https://hbr.org/2015/08/how-to-do-walking-meetings-right
4 https://twitter.com/bcredibility

Acknowledgements

Both authors

A big thank you to our former colleagues at IOV (Abel, Adolfo, Albert, Alex, Piotr, Ethan, Roman, Simon, Will, Lucas, Orkun, Carlos, Andrei, Pany, Andy, Emilia, Jackson, Misang, Victoria, Klara, Benjamin, Antoine, Karim, Isabella, Dasha, Karine, Dave and Ben, as a good friend of IOV). We learned so much about remote working by doing it. Many thanks to all those who gave their time to share their professional experience and insights, read and edit our manuscript. To all our families, the Worners, Tohmés and Villanuevas, a huge thank you for their continuous encouragement and support.

Martin

Larry, Nicole and Moustapha at Alpha Innovations for the experience of transatlantic remote working. Jochem Gerritsen, a brilliant sounding board as a remote worker. Chris van Aeken, Aleś Muchin, Shin Suri and Kuldeep Vijaykumar for their insight.

Anastasia

Martin Villanueva Ordás, beloved husband, for sharing his first-hand experience on transitioning to remote at ifeel, and for being my pillar and invaluable support throughout the whole process of writing this book. Sincere appreciation to Rolf Strom-Olsen, professor and friend, for providing encouragement and advice. To my parents, Mona and Bechara Tohmé, for their love and inspiration.

Index

PENGUIN PARTNERSHIPS

Penguin Partnerships is the Creative Sales and Promotions team at Penguin Random House. We have a long history of working with clients on a wide variety of briefs, specializing in brand promotions, bespoke publishing and retail exclusives, plus corporate, entertainment and media partnerships.

We can respond quickly to briefs and specialize in repurposing books and content for sales promotions, for use as incentives and retail exclusives as well as creating content for new books in collaboration with our partners as part of branded book relationships.

Equally if you'd simply like to buy a bulk quantity of one of our existing books at a special discount, we can help with that too. Our books can make excellent corporate or employee gifts.

Special editions, including personalized covers, excerpts of existing books or books with corporate logos can be created in large quantities for special needs.

We can work within your budget to deliver whatever you want, however you want it.

**For more information, please contact
salesenquiries@penguinrandomhouse.co.uk**